Copyright © 2014 by The Editors of Major League Baseball

All rights reserved. The use of any part of this publication reproduced, transmitted in any form or by any means, electronic, mechanical, photocopying, recording, or otherwise, or stored in a retrieval system without the prior written consent of the publisher — or, in case of photocopying or other reprographic copying, a license from the Canadian Copyright Licensing Agency — is an infringement of the copyright law.

ISBN: 978-0-7710-5739-7
Library and Archives Canada Cataloguing in Publication is available upon request

Published simultaneously in the United States of America by
Fenn/McClelland & Stewart, a division of Random House of Canada Limited, a Penguin Random House Company.

Library of Congress Control Number is available upon request

Printed and bound in the United States of America

McClelland & Stewart,
a division of Random House of Canada Limited,
a Penguin Random House Company
www.penguinrandomhouse.ca

1   2   3   4   5   18   17   16   15   14

™

CONTENTS

INTRODUCTION
THREE TIMES. FIVE YEARS. BEEN THERE, DONE THAT.

IT MAY SEEM like a world championship is old hat for San Francisco, but on Oct. 29, the Giants celebrated like it was all new.

"It's a kind of atmosphere, a kind of organization, where it's just in the blood," said Michael Morse, one of the newcomers this season. "It's in the core."

"The Poseys, the Belts, Sandovals, the Crawfords; I don't want to leave anybody out, but those are your core guys," echoed Manager Bruce Bochy, who became one of just 10 skippers in Major League history with three world titles after his club's victory this year.

In an unlikely Series that pitted against each other the American and National League Wild Card teams, who ousted the first-place Angels and Nationals, respectively, in the Division Series, dramatics were only fitting. Although the first six Fall Classic contests featured a pair of shutouts and all but one of those games was decided by five or more runs, the San Francisco Giants and Kansas City Royals found themselves knotted at three games apiece following Game 6, forcing the first seven-game duel since 2011.

While the Giants were on the verge of attaining dynasty status, the Royals were looking to win it all in their first postseason appearance in 29 years. But ace Madison Bumgarner would have none of the latter, as he stifled Kansas City's hopes, 7-1 and 5-0, respectively, in Games 1 and 5.

After his second outing, the first shutout in World Series play since 2003, teammates speculated about the possibility of Bum taking the mound again with the title on the line. "I'm sure he wouldn't deny [a chance to pitch in Game 7] if he was asked," said shortstop Brandon Crawford.

Sure enough, Bochy called on the ace left-hander after starter Tim Hudson and reliever Jeremy Affeldt combined for four innings of two-run ball. Hunter Pence contributed two hits and scored a run, and Pablo Sandoval reached base in each of his three at-bats before crossing the plate with the winning run.

Thanks to a deadly combination of strong defense and dynamic bullpen work throughout the postseason, the Giants and their core group of stars were able to claim the franchise's eighth world title, and its third since 2010.

When both teams arrived in San Francisco for Game 3, they were tied at one game apiece. But the Giants left the West Coast up 3 games to 2 before ultimately taking their third world title in five years.

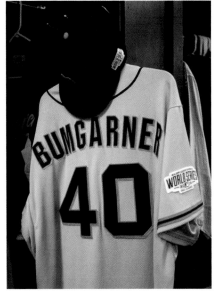

Fans donned panda heads (opposite top) in honor of Pablo "Kung Fu Panda" Sandoval, as well as festive orange gear (left). Ace Bumgarner (opposite bottom) had three strong outings over seven games to earn the World Series MVP Award.

Jean Machi, Yusmeiro Petit (opposite) and the Giants' bullpen were dominant throughout the Series. Boatloads of fans filled McCovey Cove (left) behind AT&T Park in the hopes of a splash hit. Gregor Blanco opened Game 2 with a longball.

San Francisco won its third world championship since 2010 at Kauffman Stadium, which marked the third time the Giants nabbed the title at the opposition's ballpark. World Series MVP Bumgarner (center) made the difference in his club's victory.

Posey (left) was behind the plate for each of the Series' seven games, and he later popped champagne with his teammates (below) to celebrate his third ring in five seasons with San Francisco.

HOW THE GIANTS WERE BUILT

THE GIANTS' STRETCH of three World Series titles in five seasons is testament to their core, a group that includes All-Stars Buster Posey, Madison Bumgarner and Tim Lincecum. But in today's world of free agency, players are bound to come and go. As a result, the front office must find the right supporting cast, which is precisely what San Francisco did in 2014. The bullpen was bolstered by the recent free-agent signings of pitchers Santiago Casilla and Yusmeiro Petit. As a first-year Giant, Michael Morse added pop to the lineup, while veteran Jake Peavy solidified the rotation after a midseason trade. Indeed, San Francisco has become masterful at finding the correct ingredients for Fall Classic magic.

DRAFT

Brandon Belt	5th round, 2009
Gary Brown	1st round, 2010
Madison Bumgarner	1st round, 2007
Matt Cain	1st round, 2002
Brandon Crawford	4th round, 2008
Matt Duffy	18th round, 2012
Tim Lincecum	1st round, 2006
Joe Panik	1st round, 2011
Juan Perez	13th round, 2008
Buster Posey	1st round, 2008
Sergio Romo	28th round, 2005
Andrew Susac	2nd round, 2011

WAIVERS

Hunter Strickland	selected off waivers from PIT (2013)

FREE AGENCY

Ehire Adrianza	Pre-arbitration eligible, 1 year/$501K (2014)
Jeremy Affeldt	3 years/$21M (2013)
Joaquin Arias	2 years/$2.6M (2014)
Gregor Blanco	1st-year arbitration eligible, 1 year/$2.53M (2014)
Santiago Casilla	3 years/$14M (2013)
Juan Gutierrez	2nd-year arbitration eligible, 1 year/$850K (2014)
Tim Hudson	2 years/$23M (2014)
Travis Ishikawa	1st-year arbitration eligible (2014)
Javier Lopez	3 years/$14M (2013)
Jean Machi	Pre-arbitration eligible, 1 year/$505K (2014)
Michael Morse	1 year/$6M (2014)
Angel Pagan	4 years/$45M (2013)
Yusmeiro Petit	1st-year arbitration eligible, 1 year/$845K (2014)
Hector Sanchez	Pre-arbitration eligible, 1 year/$512K (2014)
Pablo Sandoval	3rd-year arbitration eligible, 3 years/$17.15M (2012)
Ryan Vogelsong	1 year/$5M (2014)

TRADE

Jake Peavy	from BOS w/cash for Edwin Escobar and Heath Hembree (2014)
Hunter Pence	from PHI for Tommy Joseph, Seth Rosin and Nate Schierholtz (2012)

REGULAR-SEASON RESULTS

DATE	OPP.	RES.	R	RA	W-L
Monday, March 31	@ ARI	W	9	8	1-0
Tuesday, April 1	@ ARI	L	4	5	1-1
Wednesday, April 2	@ ARI	W	2	0	2-1
Thursday, April 3	@ ARI	W	8	5	3-1
Friday, April 4	@ LAD	W	8	4	4-1
Saturday, April 5	@ LAD	W	7	2	5-1
Sunday, April 6	@ LAD	L	2	6	5-2
Tuesday, April 8	ARI	W	7	3	6-2
Wednesday, April 9	ARI	L	3	7	6-3
Thursday, April 10	ARI	L	5	6	6-4
Friday, April 11	COL	W	6	5	7-4
Saturday, April 12	COL	L	0	1	7-5
Sunday, April 13	COL	W	5	4	8-5
Tuesday, April 15	LAD	W	3	2	9-5
Wednesday, April 16	LAD	W	2	1	10-5
Thursday, April 17	LAD	L	1	2	10-6
Friday, April 18	@ SD	L	1	2	10-7
Saturday, April 19	@ SD	L	1	3	10-8
Sunday, April 20	@ SD	W	4	3	11-8
Monday, April 21	@ COL	L	2	8	11-9
Tuesday, April 22	@ COL	L	1	2	11-10
Wednesday, April 23	@ COL	W	12	10	12-10
Friday, April 25	CLE	W	5	1	13-10
Saturday, April 26	CLE	W	5	3	14-10
Sunday, April 27	CLE	W	4	1	15-10
Monday, April 28	SD	L	4	6	15-11
Tuesday, April 29	SD	W	6	0	16-11
Wednesday, April 30	SD	W	3	2	17-11
Friday, May 2	@ ATL	W	2	1	18-11
Saturday, May 3	@ ATL	W	3	1	19-11
Sunday, May 4	@ ATL	W	4	1	20-11
Monday, May 5	@ PIT	W	11	10	21-11
Tuesday, May 6	@ PIT	L	1	2	21-12
Wednesday, May 7	@ PIT	L	3	4	21-13
Thursday, May 8	@ LAD	W	3	1	22-13
Friday, May 9	@ LAD	W	3	1	23-13
Saturday, May 10	@ LAD	L	2	6	23-14
Sunday, May 11	@ LAD	W	7	4	24-14
Monday, May 12	ATL	W	4	2	25-14
Tuesday, May 13	ATL	L	0	5	25-15
Wednesday, May 14	ATL	W	10	4	26-15

DATE	OPP.	RES.	R	RA	W-L
Thursday, May 15	MIA	W	6	4	27-15
Friday, May 16	MIA	L	5	7	27-16
Saturday, May 17	MIA	L	0	5	27-17
Sunday, May 18	MIA	W	4	1	28-17
Tuesday, May 20	@ COL	L	4	5	28-18
Wednesday, May 21	@ COL	W	5	1	29-18
Thursday, May 22	@ COL	W	4	2	30-18
Friday, May 23	MIN	W	6	2	31-18
Saturday, May 24	MIN	W	2	1	32-18
Sunday, May 25	MIN	W	8	1	33-18
Monday, May 26	CHC	L	4	8	33-19
Tuesday, May 27	CHC	W	4	0	34-19
Wednesday, May 28	CHC	W	5	0	35-19
Thursday, May 29	@ STL	W	6	5	36-19
Friday, May 30	@ STL	W	9	4	37-19
Saturday, May 31	@ STL	L	0	2	37-20
Sunday, June 1	@ STL	W	8	0	38-20
Tuesday, June 3	@ CIN	L	3	8	38-21
Wednesday, June 4	@ CIN	W	3	2	39-21
Thursday, June 5	@ CIN	W	6	1	40-21
Friday, June 6	NYM	W	4	2	41-21
Saturday, June 7	NYM	W	5	4	42-21
Sunday, June 8	NYM	W	6	4	43-21
Monday, June 9	WAS	L	2	9	43-22
Tuesday, June 10	WAS	L	1	2	43-23
Wednesday, June 11	WAS	L	2	6	43-24
Thursday, June 12	WAS	W	7	1	44-24
Friday, June 13	COL	L	4	7	44-25
Saturday, June 14	COL	L	4	5	44-26
Sunday, June 15	COL	L	7	8	44-27
Tuesday, June 17	@ CHW	L	2	8	44-28
Wednesday, June 18	@ CHW	L	6	7	44-29
Friday, June 20	@ ARI	L	1	4	44-30
Saturday, June 21	@ ARI	W	6	4	45-30
Sunday, June 22	@ ARI	W	4	1	46-30
Monday, June 23	SD	L	0	6	46-31
Tuesday, June 24	SD	L	2	7	46-32
Wednesday, June 25	SD	W	4	0	47-32
Thursday, June 26	CIN	L	1	3	47-33
Friday, June 27	CIN	L	2	6	47-34
Saturday, June 28	CIN	L	3	7	47-35

REGULAR-SEASON RESULTS

DATE	OPP.	RES.	R	RA	W-L
Sunday, June 29	CIN	L	0	4	47-36
Tuesday, July 1	STL	W	5	0	48-36
Wednesday, July 2	STL	L	0	2	48-37
Thursday, July 3	STL	L	2	7	48-38
Friday, July 4	@ SD	L	0	2	48-39
Saturday, July 5	@ SD	W	5	3	49-39
Sunday, July 6	@ SD	W	5	3	50-39
Monday, July 7	@ OAK	L	0	5	50-40
Tuesday, July 8	@ OAK	L	1	6	50-41
Wednesday, July 9	OAK	W	5	2	51-41
Thursday, July 10	OAK	L	1	6	51-42
Friday, July 11	ARI	W	5	0	52-42
Saturday, July 12	ARI	L	0	2	52-43
Sunday, July 13	ARI	W	8	4	53-43
Friday, July 18	@ MIA	W	9	1	54-43
Saturday, July 19	@ MIA	W	5	3	55-43
Sunday, July 20	@ MIA	L	2	3	55-44
Monday, July 21	@ PHI	W	7	4	56-44
Tuesday, July 22	@ PHI	W	9	6	57-44
Wednesday, July 23	@ PHI	W	3	1	58-44
Thursday, July 24	@ PHI	L	1	2	58-45
Friday, July 25	LAD	L	1	8	58-46
Saturday, July 26	LAD	L	0	5	58-47
Sunday, July 27	LAD	L	3	4	58-48
Monday, July 28	PIT	L	0	5	58-49
Tuesday, July 29	PIT	L	1	3	58-50
Wednesday, July 30	PIT	W	7	5	59-50
Friday, Aug. 1	@ NYM	W	5	1	60-50
Saturday, Aug. 2	@ NYM	L	2	4	60-51
Sunday, Aug. 3	@ NYM	W	9	0	61-51
Monday, Aug. 4	@ NYM	W	4	3	62-51
Tuesday, Aug. 5	@ MIL	L	3	4	62-52
Wednesday, Aug. 6	@ MIL	W	7	4	63-52
Thursday, Aug. 7	@ MIL	L	1	3	63-53
Friday, Aug. 8	@ KC	L	2	4	63-54
Saturday, Aug. 9	@ KC	L	0	5	63-55
Sunday, Aug. 10	@ KC	L	4	7	63-56
Tuesday, Aug. 12	CHW	L	2	3	63-57
Wednesday, Aug. 13	CHW	W	7	1	64-57
Friday, Aug. 15	PHI	L	3	5	64-58
Saturday, Aug. 16	PHI	W	6	5	65-58

DATE	OPP.	RES.	R	RA	W-L
Sunday, Aug. 17	PHI	W	5	2	66-58
Tuesday, Aug. 19	@ CHC	L	1	2	66-59
Wednesday, Aug. 20	@ CHC	W	8	3	67-59
Thursday, Aug. 21	@ CHC	W	5	3	68-59
Friday, Aug. 22	@ WAS	W	10	3	69-59
Saturday, Aug. 23	@ WAS	L	2	6	69-60
Sunday, Aug. 24	@ WAS	L	6	14	69-61
Monday, Aug. 25	COL	L	2	3	69-62
Tuesday, Aug. 26	COL	W	3	0	70-62
Wednesday, Aug. 27	COL	W	4	2	71-62
Thursday, Aug. 28	COL	W	4	1	72-62
Friday, Aug. 29	MIL	W	13	2	73-62
Saturday, Aug. 30	MIL	W	3	1	74-62
Sunday, Aug. 31	MIL	W	15	5	75-62
Monday, Sept. 1	@ COL	L	9	10	75-63
Tuesday, Sept. 2	@ COL	W	12	7	76-63
Wednesday, Sept. 3	@ COL	L	2	9	76-64
Friday, Sept. 5	@ DET	W	8	2	77-64
Saturday, Sept. 6	@ DET	W	5	4	78-64
Sunday, Sept. 7	@ DET	L	1	6	78-65
Tuesday, Sept. 9	ARI	W	5	1	79-65
Wednesday, Sept. 10	ARI	W	5	0	80-65
Thursday, Sept. 11	ARI	W	6	2	81-65
Friday, Sept. 12	LAD	W	9	0	82-65
Saturday, Sept. 13	LAD	L	0	17	82-66
Sunday, Sept. 14	LAD	L	2	4	82-67
Monday, Sept. 15	@ ARI	L	2	6	82-68
Tuesday, Sept. 16	@ ARI	W	2	1	83-68
Wednesday, Sept. 17	@ ARI	W	4	2	84-68
Friday, Sept. 19	@ SD	L	0	5	84-69
Saturday, Sept. 20	@ SD	L	2	3	84-70
Sunday, Sept. 21	@ SD	L	2	8	84-71
Monday, Sept. 22	@ LAD	W	5	2	85-71
Tuesday, Sept. 23	@ LAD	L	2	4	85-72
Wednesday, Sept. 24	@ LAD	L	1	9	85-73
Thursday, Sept. 25	SD	W	9	8	86-73
Friday, Sept. 26	SD	L	1	4	86-74
Saturday, Sept. 27	SD	W	3	1	87-74
Sunday, Sept. 28	SD	W	9	3	88-74

REGULAR-SEASON STATS

NO.	PLAYER	B/T	W	L	ERA	SO	BB	SV	BIRTHDATE	BIRTHPLACE
PITCHERS										
41	Jeremy Affeldt	L/L	4	2	2.28	41	14	0	6/6/79	Phoenix, AZ
40	Madison Bumgarner	R/L	18	10	2.98	219	43	0	8/1/89	Hickory, NC
18	Matt Cain	R/R	2	7	4.18	70	32	0	10/1/84	Dothan, AL
46	Santiago Casilla	R/R	3	3	1.70	45	15	19	7/25/80	San Cristobal, D.R.
57	Juan Gutierrez	R/R	1	2	3.96	44	16	0	7/14/83	Puerto la Cruz, Venezuela
17	Tim Hudson	R/R	9	13	3.57	120	34	0	7/14/75	Columbus, GA
55	Tim Lincecum	L/R	12	9	4.74	134	63	1	6/15/84	Bellevue, WA
49	Javier Lopez	L/L	1	1	3.11	22	19	0	7/11/77	San Juan, Puerto Rico
63	Jean Machi	R/R	7	1	2.58	51	18	2	2/1/82	El Tigre, Venezuela
22	Jake Peavy	R/R	7	13	3.73	158	63	0	5/31/81	Mobile, AL
52	Yusmeiro Petit	R/R	5	5	3.69	133	22	0	11/22/84	Maracaibo, Venezuela
54	Sergio Romo	R/R	6	4	3.72	59	12	23	3/4/83	Brawley, CA
60	Hunter Strickland	R/R	1	0	0.00	9	0	1	9/24/88	Thomaston, GA
32	Ryan Vogelsong	R/R	8	13	4.00	151	58	0	7/22/77	Charlotte, NC

NO.	PLAYER	B/T	AB	H	AVG	HR	RBI	OBP	BIRTHDATE	BIRTHPLACE
CATCHERS										
28	Buster Posey	R/R	547	170	.311	22	89	.364	3/27/87	Leesburg, GA
29	Hector Sanchez	S/R	163	32	.196	3	28	.237	11/17/89	Maracay, Venezuela
34	Andrew Susac	R/R	88	24	.273	3	19	.326	3/22/90	Roseville, CA
INFIELDERS										
6	Ehire Adrianza	S/R	97	23	.237	0	5	.279	8/21/89	Guarenas, Venezuela
13	Joaquin Arias	R/R	193	49	.254	0	15	.281	9/21/84	Santo Domingo, D.R.
9	Brandon Belt	L/L	214	52	.243	12	27	.306	4/20/88	Nacogdoches, TX
35	Brandon Crawford	L/R	491	121	.246	10	69	.324	1/21/87	Mountain View, CA
50	Matt Duffy	R/R	60	16	.267	0	8	.302	1/15/91	Long Beach, CA
45	Travis Ishikawa	L/L	107	27	.252	3	18	.311	9/24/83	Seattle, WA
12	Joe Panik	L/R	269	82	.305	1	18	.343	10/30/90	Yonkers, NY
48	Pablo Sandoval	S/R	588	164	.279	16	73	.324	8/11/86	Puerto Cabello, Venezuela
OUTFIELDERS										
7	Gregor Blanco	L/L	393	102	.260	5	38	.333	12/24/83	Caracas, Venezuela
56	Gary Brown	R/R	7	3	.429	0	1	.429	9/28/88	Diamond Bar, CA
38	Michael Morse	R/R	438	122	.279	16	61	.336	3/22/82	Fort Lauderdale, FL
16	Angel Pagan	S/R	383	115	.300	3	27	.342	7/2/81	Rio Piedras, P.R.
8	Hunter Pence	R/R	650	180	.277	20	74	.332	4/13/83	Fort Worth, TX
2	Juan Perez	R/R	100	17	.170	1	3	.224	11/13/86	Santiago, D.R.

Manager: Bruce Bochy (15). Coaches: Tim Flannery (1), Mark Gardner (26), Roberto Kelly (39),
Hensley Meulens (31), Dave Righetti (33), Ron Wotus (23).

OCT. 1

GIANTS 8, PIRATES 0

ENTERING THE WILD CARD matchup, Giants ace Madison Bumgarner knew that he would have to bring his best stuff to this must-win contest. Against the Pittsburgh Pirates, Bumgarner dazzled, keeping the Bucs off balance in an 8-0 complete-game shutout. Josh Harrison was the only Pirates hitter to challenge the hurler, tallying two of Pittsburgh's four hits.

While Bumgarner was the star of the night, he had plenty of support. Edinson Volquez, the Pirates' starter, matched his counterpart through the first three innings, but Brandon Crawford took the air out of PNC Park in the fourth, when he became the first shortstop in MLB post-season history to hit a grand slam. Brandon Belt tacked on three runs with a pair of singles in the sixth and seventh innings. Buster Posey added the visitors' final run in the eighth, while rookie Joe Panik had a standout showing, as well, going 3 for 5 in the contest.

Once Bumgarner struck out his 10th batter of the night for the second out of the ninth, Giants faithful stood in enemy territory to watch the final out, knowing that the postseason was only just beginning.

	1	2	3	4	5	6	7	8	9	R	H	E
SAN FRANCISCO	0	0	0	4	0	1	2	1	0	8	11	2
PITTSBURGH	0	0	0	0	0	0	0	0	0	0	4	0

WP: Bumgarner LP: Volquez
HR: SF: Crawford

In the Giants' second ever Wild Card berth, ace Bumgarner pitched a complete-game shutout to earn his team a spot in the NLDS.

Crawford and Belt both contributed to San Francisco's domination in Pittsburgh, combining for three hits and seven RBI.

"IT'S REALLY HARD TO PITCH A BETTER GAME THAN WHAT MADISON DID. WE HAD THE RIGHT GUY OUT THERE AND HE EXECUTED ALL NIGHT AGAINST A TOUGH LINEUP. IT'S TOUGH TO WIN HERE IN PITTSBURGH. BUT WHEN MADISON'S ON THE MOUND, WE HAVE ALL THE CONFIDENCE IN THE WORLD, AND HE SET THE TONE EARLY." *Bruce Bochy*

GAME 1, OCT. 3

GIANTS 3, NATIONALS 2

MADISON BUMGARNER'S DOMINANT performance in the Wild Card Game left the Giants' pitching staff fresh for the start of the NLDS. Jake Peavy tossed 5.2 innings of shutout ball, and five relievers finished off a 3-2 win against the Nationals in Game 1.

The same heroes from the Wild Card Game produced again, as Joe Panik went 2 for 5 with an RBI and a triple, Brandon Crawford collected three hits and Brandon Belt drove in a run on two base knocks. Travis Ishikawa added a run scored in the top of the third, too.

The sixth inning may have been the defining frame, though. After Peavy gave up a double and a walk with two outs sandwiched in between, Manager Bruce Bochy pulled him. His replacement, Javier Lopez, walked the next batter to load the bases, though, so Bochy then turned to rookie reliever Hunter Strickland to get out of the jam. Strickland lived up to the occasion, getting Washington's Ian Desmond to strike out swinging. Despite two home runs in the seventh inning by Bryce Harper and Asdrubal Cabrera, Giants closer Santiago Casilla wrapped up the win on the road.

	1	2	3	4	5	6	7	8	9	R	H	E
SAN FRANCISCO	0	0	1	1	0	0	1	0	0	3	12	0
WASHINGTON	0	0	0	0	0	0	2	0	0	2	6	0

WP: Peavy **LP:** Strasburg **SV:** Casilla
HR: WAS: Harper, Cabrera

Buster Posey, San Francisco's star catcher and former NL MVP, singled in the seventh to bring Panik home and increase the Giants' lead to 3-0.

The NLCS opened at Nationals Park with Peavy (right) throwing 5.2 innings of shutout ball in the fourth Division Series start of his 13-year career.

"AS A COMPETITOR, YOU ALWAYS WANT TO HELP THE TEAM WIN. SINCE I CAME UP, I WANTED TO BE ANOTHER LINK IN THE CHAIN. THAT IS HOW THIS TEAM IS. THERE IS NOT ONE GUY THAT WE HAVE TO RELY ON; IT'S THE ENTIRE TEAM." *Joe Panik*

GAME 2, OCT. 4 GIANTS 2, NATIONALS 1

THE GIANTS AND Nationals began their Game 2 endurance test just past 5:30 p.m. ET. When it ended six hours and 23 minutes later, it clocked in as the longest game ever played in postseason history.

It started as a pitcher's duel. San Francisco's Tim Hudson went 7.1 innings, giving up just one run in the third inning. Nationals starter Jordan Zimmermann shut down the Giants for 8.2 innings, yet San Francisco refused to surrender. With two outs in the ninth, rookie Joe Panik drew a walk, and after a pitching change, a Buster Posey single put runners on first and second. Pablo Sandoval doubled to score Panik, and the Nationals managed to nab Posey at the plate by inches.

The game then stretched for another eight scoreless innings, with pitching keeping the bats at bay. San Francisco's Yusmeiro Petit came on in very late, and long, relief, striking out seven and allowing only a single hit in six innings. Petit was rewarded for his efforts, as Brandon Belt deposited a home run into the right-field seats in the top of the 18th inning to put the Giants ahead. In the bottom of the frame, rookie Hunter Strickland got Jayson Werth to line out to center to secure the win.

	1	2	3	4	5	6	7	8	9	10	11	12	13	14	15	16	17	18	R	H	E
SAN FRANCISCO	0	0	0	0	0	0	0	0	1	0	0	0	0	0	0	0	0	1	**2**	**8**	**0**
WASHINGTON	0	0	0	1	0	0	0	0	0	0	0	0	0	0	0	0	0	0	**1**	**9**	**0**

WP: Petit LP: Roark SV: Strickland HR: SF: Belt

Sandoval doubled off Drew Storen in the top of the ninth to bring Panik home.

Petit got the win after going six innings and allowing just one hit.

Wilson Ramos tagged out Posey at home in the top of the ninth, preventing the go-ahead run from scoring. The game continued for nine more innings.

"I DON'T THINK THE MOMENT EVER GETS TOO BIG FOR US. WE DON'T GET AHEAD OF OURSELVES. WE DON'T TRY TO DO TOO MUCH. IT SEEMS LIKE WE PLAY OUR BEST BASEBALL WHEN IT GETS INTO PLAYOFF TIME. WE PLAY, WE DON'T TRY TO UP GO UP AND DO TOO MUCH, GET THAT BIG HOME RUN. IT'S NOT NECESSARILY ABOUT BEING A HERO, IT'S ABOUT BEING A TEAM." *Brandon Belt*

GAME 3, OCT. 6

NATIONALS 4, GIANTS 1

WHEN THE NATIONALS traded for Doug Fister in the off-season, they were hoping for a ground ball machine who wasn't afraid of the big game spotlight. With the season on the line, Fister unleashed seven innings of shutout stuff, outdueling Giants ace Madison Bumgarner and lowering his overall postseason ERA to a stellar 2.60.

Bumgarner was also sharp that night, and the left-hander matched Fister inning for inning until the seventh, when the game unraveled. After Bumgarner gave up a leadoff single to Ian Desmond and a walk to Bryce Harper, Wilson Ramos bunted on an 0-2 pitch. Bumgarner charged the ball but fired wildly to third base. The throw was out of Pablo Sandoval's reach, and both Desmond and Harper came around to score on the error. Asdrubal

Cabrera then drove Wilson Ramos home, and although Bumgarner retired the next three batters, he left the game trailing by three runs.

In the top of the ninth, Bryce Harper went deep, adding insurance for the Nats. Despite giving up two hits and a run in the ninth, Nationals closer Drew Storen recovered to secure Washington's first win in the series.

	1	2	3	4	5	6	7	8	9	R	H	E
WASHINGTON	0	0	0	0	0	0	3	0	1	4	7	0
SAN FRANCISCO	0	0	0	0	0	0	0	0	1	1	6	1

WP: Fister LP: Bumgarner
HR: WAS: Harper

Harper scored on Bumgarner's error in the seventh, one of the outfielder's two runs in the contest, en route to a 4-1 Nationals victory.

Bumgarner and Fister dueled for seven innings in Game 3, but despite his six K's, the Giants' ace came out on the losing end.

"IT'S SUCH AN INTENSE GAME, AND I KNOW THEY WANT TO GET THAT OUT AT THIRD BASE, BUT THEY PROBABLY TRIED TO DO A LITTLE TOO MUCH THERE. THEY PLAYED SO WELL. WE MADE A MISTAKE. WE'VE GOT TO LEARN FROM IT. BUT, YOU KNOW, WE'VE GOT TO MOVE ON." *Bruce Bochy*

GAME 4, OCT. 7

GIANTS 3, NATIONALS 2

THE GIANTS HAD a knack for winning this postseason, no matter how quirky the process. While timely hitting and great pitching had propelled the Giants to a 2-games-to-1 series lead, it was heads-up baserunning and eye-popping defense that secured the club's chance to play in its third NLCS in five seasons.

San Francisco grabbed an early lead in the second inning after a bases-loaded walk and RBI groundout that scored Brandon Crawford and Juan Perez. Starter Ryan Vogelsong responded with 5.2 innings of one-run ball, giving up only an RBI double to Bryce Harper that plated Ian Desmond in the fifth. Hunter Pence provided stellar defense in right field, robbing Jayson Werth, the last batter that Vogelsong faced, of an extra-base hit, by hurling his body against the outfield wall to catch the drive.

Harper would tie the game in the seventh, as he launched a blast off Hunter Strickland into McCovey Cove, but San Francisco refused to quit. The Giants even had luck on their side. In the bottom of the inning, they loaded the bases and, with Pablo Sandoval at the plate, capitalized on an Aaron Barrett wild pitch, as Joe Panik scored what proved to be the winning run. The Giants held on to win 3-2 and advance to another championship series.

	1	2	3	4	5	6	7	8	9	R	H	E
WASHINGTON	0	0	0	0	1	0	1	0	0	2	4	1
SAN FRANCISCO	0	2	0	0	0	0	1	0	-	3	9	0

WP: Strickland LP: Thornton SV: Casilla
HR: WAS: Harper

The Giants finished up the NLDS on their home turf before heading to St. Louis, where they would win their 23rd pennant.

With Sandoval (left) at the plate, Panik took advantage of a wild pitch by Barrett, scoring what would prove to be the game-winning run in the bottom of the seventh.

"WHAT MAKES THIS PLACE SPECIAL IS THAT WE'RE VERY UNIFIED. THERE'S NOT ONE GUY TRYING TO SHINE BRIGHTER THAN THE NEXT. IT'S ALL PULLING ON THE SAME ROPE FOR THE SAME CAUSE AT THE SAME TIME, AND IT'S FUN. WE'RE ABLE TO INCORPORATE THE FANS HERE AT HOME, THE SOLD-OUT CROWDS. IT'S HARD TO NOT REWARD THEM BY PLAYING HARD AND GIVING IT YOUR BEST." *Sergio Romo*

The Giants took champagne showers in the AT&T Park clubhouse after they clinched the NLDS in four games.

"[PENCE] MAKES A GREAT CATCH AT SOME POINT EVERY TIME I'M PITCHING IN THE POSTSEASON. AND THANK GOODNESS HE DID, BECAUSE THAT'S PROBABLY A TRIPLE IF HE DOESN'T CATCH THAT BALL. SO HE'S THE MAN." *Ryan Vogelsong*

Pence stopped the Nationals in their tracks throughout the series thanks to his agility and stunning grabs.

GAME 1, OCT. 11   GIANTS 3, CARDINALS 0

IN GAME 1 at Busch Stadium, Madison Bumgarner was again his dominant self, setting a record for the most consecutive scoreless innings pitched on the road in postseason play. He surrendered a single to Matt Carpenter to start the game, but retired 10 of the next 11 batters he faced, giving San Francisco's offense a chance to take an early lead.

The Giants did just that in the second inning. Pablo Sandoval doubled to open the frame, Hunter Pence followed with a walk and Brandon Belt singled to load the bases. Adam Wainwright struck out Brandon Crawford, but St. Louis wasn't out of the jam yet, as Travis Ishikawa blooped a single to knock in Sandoval. Bumgarner then lined out, but third baseman Matt Carpenter gifted the Giants their second run by committing an error on Gregor Blanco's hard grounder. This would prove to be all the scoring that San Francisco needed.

Bumgarner went on to allow just four hits while tallying seven K's over 7.2 innings. Belt added the final run of the game on a sacrifice fly in the third, and Sergio Romo and Santiago Casilla closed out the game in scoreless fashion to put San Francisco ahead in the series.

	1	2	3	4	5	6	7	8	9	R	H	E
SAN FRANCISCO	0	2	1	0	0	0	0	0	0	3	8	0
ST. LOUIS	0	0	0	0	0	0	0	0	0	0	4	1

WP: Bumgarner   LP: Wainwright   SV: Casilla

Bumgarner continued his near-flawless work in his third start of the 2014 postseason. He faced 29 batters over 7.2 innings.

Ishikawa's diving grab in the fourth inning robbed Yadier Molina of a hit and kept the Cardinals off the board.

"[MADISON BUMGARNER] WAS ON TOP OF HIS GAME, HITTING SPOTS, USING ALL HIS PITCHES. HE'S SO GOOD AT WHAT HE DOES. THIS KID, SINCE HE'S COME UP, HE'S JUST GOTTEN BETTER." *Bruce Bochy*

Sandoval's leadoff double in the second yielded a three-hit, two-run outburst, during which eight Giants came to the plate.

"MAN, [IT'S] EXCITING TO PLAY IN OCTOBER, YOU KNOW. LAST YEAR, I WAS HOME WATCHING THE GAMES ON TV. NOW IT'S WIN OR GO HOME." *Pablo Sandoval*

San Francisco's Game 1 win was a team-wide effort, as five of the eight starting position players contributed hits.

Bumgarner's Best

NOT EVERY POSTSEASON includes the breaking of an MLB record set 90 years ago, but San Francisco's Madison Bumgarner did just that in NLCS Game 1. The Giants' ace set a new mark for the most consecutive scoreless innings pitched on the road in postseason play (26.2), surpassing the previous record set by Art Nehf of the New York Giants from 1921–24. Bumgarner's shutout performance into the fifth inning set the new benchmark, as he last gave up a postseason run on the road in the fifth frame of the 2010 NLCS against the Phillies. He also became the first pitcher in MLB history with three straight scoreless postseason starts on the road, and earned a 2.58 ERA between all career postseason games through Oct. 11. Only 16 pitchers in MLB history have ever thrown 20 or more consecutive scoreless innings in the postseason.

GAME 2, OCT. 12

CARDINALS 5, GIANTS 4

EVEN IN THE face of adversity, the Cardinals managed to soar.

Matt Carpenter put the Redbirds on the board in Game 2 with a home run off Jake Peavy in the bottom of the third inning, and Randal Grichuk singled with the bases loaded in the fourth to help St. Louis increase its early lead. The Cardinals' advantage evaporated, though, after the Giants scored in the fifth, sixth and seventh innings, thanks to strategic small ball from Joaquin Arias, Hunter Pence and Gregor Blanco. To make matters worse, St. Louis's fearless catcher, Yadier Molina, was removed from the game in the bottom of the sixth inning after straining his oblique during an at-bat. Tony Cruz replaced Molina, who was visibly in pain, in the top of the seventh.

Rather than losing hope, the Cardinals rallied. To the delight of a hometown crowd, rookie Oscar Taveras homered in the bottom of the seventh to tie the game, and Matt Adams launched a longball in the eighth to retake the lead. Finally, after the Giants tied the game in the top of the ninth, Kolten Wong drove the second pitch he saw over the right-field wall, and the Cardinals won in walk-off fashion.

	1	2	3	4	5	6	7	8	9	R	H	E
SAN FRANCISCO	0	0	0	0	1	1	1	0	1	4	10	0
ST. LOUIS	0	0	1	1	0	0	1	1	1	5	8	0

WP: Maness **LP:** Romo
HR: STL: Carpenter, Taveras, Adams, Wong

Matt Duffy took advantage of a Trevor Rosenthal wild pitch in the ninth to tie the game, but the Giants weren't able to take the lead.

Peavy allowed a mere two runs in his second postseason start as a Giant, but the deficit proved too much for San Francisco to surmount.

"YOU HAVE SO MUCH ADRENALINE, SO MUCH EXCITEMENT AT THIS STAGE THAT THINGS ARE GOING TO HAPPEN. THAT'S THE BEAUTY OF BASEBALL. THINGS YOU NEVER EXPECT TO HAPPEN, HAPPEN." *Kolten Wong*

GAME 3, OCT. 14

GIANTS 5, CARDINALS 4

GAME 3 OF the NLCS marked just the eighth time in Major League history that a playoff game ended on an error. After squandering an early lead, the Giants won the contest on an errant throw in extra innings.

San Francisco got to John Lackey quickly, as Buster Posey and Pablo Sandoval both singled with two outs in the first. Hunter Pence then doubled home Posey, and Travis Ishikawa added three more runs with a double of his own one batter later.

The Cardinals chipped away at the Giants' four-run lead via a Kolten Wong two-run triple in the fourth and two more RBI in the sixth and seventh. The game remained tied through the ninth, but in the 10th inning, it quickly unraveled. Brandon Crawford led off the bottom of the frame with an eight-pitch walk. Juan Perez followed with a single, and when Gregor Blanco attempted to bunt the runners over, Choate threw the ball wide of first. Crawford hustled home with the game-winning run.

	1	2	3	4	5	6	7	8	9	10	R	H	E
ST. LOUIS	0	0	0	2	0	1	1	0	0	0	4	9	1
SAN FRANCISCO	4	0	0	0	0	0	0	0	0	1	5	8	0

WP: Romo LP: Choate
HR: STL: Grichuk

Blanco's 10th-inning bunt attempt was successful, as Choate airmailed the throw to first, allowing the winning run to score.

Crawford drew a free pass to open the 10th, and it came around to hurt St. Louis, as he scored the game winner on Choate's error.

"IT'S A DREAM COME TRUE. IT SOUNDS LIKE A CLICHE, BUT WHEN I WAS 5, I WAS HOPING THAT I WOULD BE THE SHORTSTOP ON THE GIANTS ONE DAY. JUST TO BE HERE IS AWESOME. IT'S LITERALLY A DREAM COME TRUE, AND TO BE FIGHTING FOR ANOTHER WORLD SERIES WOULD JUST BE EXTRA ICING ON THE CAKE." *Brandon Crawford*

In his fifth season with the Giants, Ishikawa proved valuable at the plate, going 1 for 3 with three RBI in Game 3.

Jon Jay, who debuted for St. Louis in 2010, made a handful of dramatic diving catches in the series's early games to keep the Cards competitive.

A Game 3 win at AT&T Park ignited a frenzy of excitement for players and fans alike, and kept the series alive in San Francisco for Games 4 and 5.

GAME 4, OCT. 15

GIANTS 6, CARDINALS 4

THE SAN FRANCISCO Giants used a combination of impressive defense and timely hits to come back from an early deficit in Game 4 to take a 3-games-to-1 series lead over St. Louis.

The Giants and Cardinals both scored runs in the first inning, and in the second, A.J. Pierzynski put his club ahead on an RBI single. The Redbirds led off the third with a double and a single, but Pablo Sandoval prevented any major damage by turning an amazing double play from his knees, allowing only one run to score. Kolten Wong added another with a home run before the frame ended. Two-out RBI singles by Buster Posey and Hunter Pence in the bottom of the third quickly brought the Giants back within just one run.

That all changed in the sixth. San Francisco's rally began with a Juan Perez walk and a Brandon Crawford single. Gregor Blanco reached base on a fielder's choice, which scored Perez, and Joe Panik drove in Crawford on a groundout. Posey followed with another two-out single. Once the Giants finished scoring, Yusmeiro Petit and the rest of the 'pen shut out the Birds for the final six innings.

	1	2	3	4	5	6	7	8	9	R	H	E
ST. LOUIS	1	1	2	0	0	0	0	0	0	4	11	0
SAN FRANCISCO	1	0	2	0	0	3	0	0	-	6	11	0

WP: Petit LP: Gonzales SV: Casilla
HR: STL: Wong

Posey's sac fly scored Blanco in the first, and he then added a single to bring Joaquin Arias home in the third for two of his three RBI in Game 4.

Santiago Casilla struck out two Cardinals in the ninth, serving up a scoreless inning and earning the save.

"A LOT OF GUYS WERE ON THIS TEAM IN 2012, WHEN WE WERE IN THE SAME BOAT THAT THE CARDINALS ARE IN AND WERE ABLE TO WIN THREE IN A ROW. WE'RE DEFINITELY NOT TAKING ANYTHING FOR GRANTED."

Buster Posey

Petit, who led a dominant Giants bullpen throughout the NLCS, authored three scoreless innings with four strikeouts and gave up just one hit.

"THAT'S QUITE A COMEBACK, AND IT ALL STARTS WITH PETIT. YOU KNOW, HE GIVES YOU A CHANCE TO COME BACK, AND ALSO ALLOWS YOU TO STILL HAVE THE GUYS THAT YOU WANT TO USE LATE IN THE BALLGAME. SO PETIT SAVED US TONIGHT WITH HIS EFFORT." *Bruce Bochy*

In his second postseason following an August 2013 debut, Wong contributed a combined six RBI and three homers through Game 4.

GAME 5, OCT. 16

GIANTS 6, CARDINALS 3

TRAVIS ISHIKAWA MAY have just 22 regular-season home runs in his seven-year career, but after Game 5, he could claim one of the most memorable blasts in Giants postseason history.

Fans at AT&T Park were prepared to witness a pitchers' duel between two of the National League's premier aces, Adam Wainwright and Madison Bumgarner, and neither disappointed. Wainwright struck out seven over seven innings while allowing just two runs on a Joe Panik homer in the bottom of the third. Bumgarner gave up an RBI double to Jon Jay in the third, as well as home runs to Matt Adams and Tony Cruz in the next frame, but the soon-to-be NLCS MVP settled down to retire the final 13 batters he faced.

In the eighth inning, Michael Morse promptly tied the game with a home run over the left-field wall. Jeremy Affeldt pitched out of a bases-loaded jam in the top of the ninth, and in the bottom frame, after a Pablo Sandoval single and a Brandon Belt walk, Ishikawa crushed the third pitch he saw into the right-field stands, sending the Giants to their third Fall Classic in five years.

	1	2	3	4	5	6	7	8	9	R	H	E
ST. LOUIS	0	0	1	2	0	0	0	0	0	3	6	0
SAN FRANCISCO	0	0	2	0	0	0	0	1	3	6	7	0

WP: Affeldt LP: Wacha
HR: STL: Adams, Cruz SF: Ishikawa, Morse, Panik

Affeldt forced Oscar Taveras to ground out in the top on the ninth, preventing the go-ahead run from scoring, before the Giants came back to win it all.

Game 5 ended when outfielder Ishikawa sent a Michael Wacha pitch into deep right field, scoring three.

"I DON'T REMEMBER TOUCHING THIRD. I DON'T REMEMBER TOUCHING HOME. THE LAST THING I REMEMBER WAS BEING THROWN DOWN AND MY JERSEY BEING RIPPED OFF. I WAS JUST SO OUT OF BREATH FROM YELLING AND SCREAMING, AND I HAD TO HAVE GUYS HELP ME STAND BACK UP TO FINISH CELEBRATING." *Travis Ishikawa*

Morse restored hope for a Game 5 clinch with an eighth-inning homer that tied the score and paved the way for a three-run Giants ninth.

Kung-Fu Moves

TYPICALLY KNOWN FOR his bat skills in October (his 14-game postseason hitting streak marks the longest in franchise history), Giants third baseman Pablo Sandoval added solid defense to his postseason resume this year. Sandoval kicked off the Giants' World Series run by making a leaping catch and flipping over the Pirates dugout rail at PNC Park to nab a Russell Martin foul ball in the seventh inning of the NL Wild Card Game. In the NLCS, Panda made a diving catch to prevent St. Louis from scoring a tie-breaking, go-ahead run in the 10th inning of Game 3.

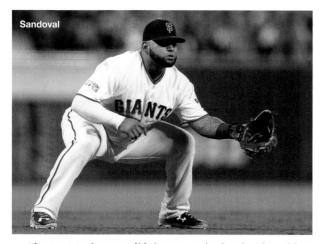

Sandoval

The 2010 Series MVP didn't go unnoticed at the plate either. Sandoval finished the NLCS with a .400 average, eight hits and three doubles. Through the 2014 NLCS, Panda had reached base safely in 24 consecutive postseason games, proving that his dominance this year reflects his October consistency.

"I COULDN'T BE HAPPIER FOR [ISHIKAWA]. I MEAN, IT WAS A GUTSY EFFORT THROUGH ALL THIS, AND I COULDN'T BE PROUDER OF THESE GUYS. THEY JUST DON'T STOP FIGHTING. WE KNOW WE HAVE A LOT OF WORK AHEAD OF US AND WE'RE PLAYING A GREAT TEAM. BUT TO GET TO THIS POINT, IT'S TIME TO CELEBRATE." *Bruce Bochy*

Ishikawa (opposite) mashed a walk-off homer in the bottom of the ninth in Game 5 before Bumgarner (above, left) was named the NLCS MVP for his 15.2 innings of nine-hit ball throughout the series. Hysteria ensued on and off the field as the club celebrated its third World Series berth since 2010.

GAME 1, OCT. 21

GIANTS 7, ROYALS 1

THE KAUFFMAN STADIUM crowd was electric as the Royals' first World Series game since 1985 rolled into Kansas City, but the Giants silenced the hometown faithful quickly, jumping out to a 3-0 first-inning lead.

Gregor Blanco helped his team get to starter James Shields early, leading off the game with a single. Buster Posey followed with a base knock two batters later, and cleanup hitter Pablo Sandoval doubled for his first of two hits on the night. The blast looked like it would drive in two, but right fielder Nori Aoki got the ball in quickly, allowing Omar Infante to nail Posey at the plate on the relay. The saved run was big for Kansas City, as San Francisco's ebullient outfielder Hunter Pence drilled a two-run homer to deep center field when he stepped to the plate next.

"I didn't even know the ball could go that far, especially in this ballpark," Sandoval said. "We were excited."

The Giants' assault continued, as Shields lasted just three innings, surrendering five earned runs on seven hits. The Royals' relief corps of Danny Duffy, Tim Collins and Jason Frasor minimized the damage to just four more hits and two runs, but the worst of it was done by the time Duffy took the mound in the fourth. "They make you grind," Duffy said. "It's a very good lineup and a very good team."

A Salvador Perez solo home run in the bottom of the seventh put the Royals on the board, but a comeback was nowhere in sight.

"When you have your ace on the mound and you give him some early run support, that's always a positive," said pitcher Jeremy Affeldt. "[Winning] Game 1 is important because you're guaranteed at least a split going back to your place. You never want to be behind the eight ball right out of the gate. They had momentum, so to get Game 1 was huge."

Huge may be an understatement. The last time the Giants were in the Series, they rallied for an 8-3, Game 1 drubbing of the Tigers in 2012, and ultimately swept Detroit. They also scored 11 runs in their Game 1 W against the Rangers in 2010, a Series they won in five. Before 2014, only one team in the past three decades (the '96 Braves) had won Game 1 of the Fall Classic by six or more runs and did not win the Series.

	1	2	3	4	5	6	7	8	9	R	H	E
SAN FRANCISCO	3	0	0	2	0	0	2	0	0	7	11	1
KANSAS CITY	0	0	0	0	0	0	1	0	0	1	4	0

WP: Bumgarner LP: Shields
HR: SF: Pence KC: Perez

Despite changes in the lineup over the years, the Giants started off their third World Series in five years in dominant fashion with a 7-1, Game 1 victory.

NLCS MVP Madison Bumgarner started off the World Series with a seven-inning performance that included five K's and an 0.57 WHIP.

"[BUMGARNER] IS A GUY THAT IS ABLE TO ELEVATE HIS GAME. HE'S EXTREMELY COMPETITIVE. YOU DEFINITELY FEEL GOOD WITH HIM ON THE MOUND, BUT I DON'T THINK ANYBODY RELAXED." *Buster Posey*

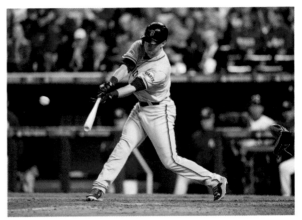

"[SANDOVAL] SEEMS LIKE HE COULD GO 10 FOR 10 WHEN HE'S UP THERE. HE CARRIES THIS TEAM, AND HE'S OBVIOUSLY HOT RIGHT NOW."
Brandon Belt

Sandoval (bottom right) knocked a double in the first and later celebrated with Belt (above). Joe Panik tripled in the seventh to give his club a six-run lead.

Pence mashed the first home run of the Series in the top of the first to set the tone for the rest of the game.

A Wild Pair

WHEN THE GIANTS and Royals squared off in this year's Fall Classic, it was just the second all–Wild Card World Series matchup in history. They combined for 177 regular-season wins, the fourth-fewest ever (and two of the previous three instances came during shortened seasons). Yet, don't try to tell any of their October opponents that San Francisco or Kansas City represented an easy draw. Getting hot at precisely the right time and playing their best baseball when they needed to most, they entered the World Series with a combined 16-2 postseason record (8-2 for the Giants, 8-0 for the Royals).

"It's a tough road, and you're going through some good clubs," Giants Manager Bruce Bochy said. "We had to go through Washington and St. Louis. Our guys have amazed me. You do sometimes look and say we're pretty blessed to have a group of guys that just seemed determined to get here."

The Game 1 victory marked the Giants' seventh-straight World Series win, dating back to Game 4 in 2010. The Royals, on the other hand, had no reason to hit the panic button, as they lost the first two games of the 1985 World Series, only to storm back and defeat the Cardinals in seven during the club's last Fall Classic appearance. The 2014 edition of the Royals also kept in mind the fact that they are the only team ever to win its first eight postseason games in any given year. "The way it all has unfolded, I think this was a case where being the Wild Card ended up working to our advantage," said Royals Manager Ned Yost. "That win over Oakland in the Wild Card Game showed our guys that they could win [in the postseason]. If we didn't win that game, I'm not so sure we could have gone on to sweep the next two series."

When it comes to win totals, these clubs may not have racked them up in the regular season, but they proved they know how to claim victory in October. And they realized as the World Series began that only one win total still matters: four — that's the number it takes to win the world title.

GAME 2, OCT. 22

ROYALS 7, GIANTS 2

AFTER A CRUSHING Game 1 loss, the young Royals made a statement in Game 2, bouncing back to drop the Giants, 7-2, and even the Series at one game apiece. Things began ominously for the Royals, as San Francisco leadoff hitter Gregor Blanco crushed a Yordano Ventura 98-mph fastball into the right-field seats for a quick, 1-0 Giants lead. But instead of succumbing to a "here we go again" worry, the Royals answered right back. A two-out RBI single by Billy Butler in the first and a two-out RBI single by Alcides Escobar in the second tied the score and gave the Royals their first lead of the Series, respectively. "We're a very aggressive team," Lorenzo Cain said, "and we were swinging tonight."

After the Giants tied the game in the fourth, Kansas City's bats exploded for a five-run sixth inning to chase starter Jake Peavy, rattle three relievers and put the game away. A two-run double by Salvador Perez and a two-run homer by Omar Infante provided the largest fireworks, both on the scoreboard and the field. As Perez touched home on Infante's homer, tempers ignited. Giants reliever Hunter Strickland, who apparently became enraged after giving up his fifth longball of the postseason, began yelling at Perez, and players needed to be separated. "I was just happy," Perez said. "Then he yelled as I scored. He said, 'Let's go,' or something. I don't want to fight anybody on the field."

The flareups — both Strickland's comments and the bullpen implosion — were out of character for the usually even-keel Giants. "He's an intense kid, and it probably got away from him a little bit," Manager Bruce Bochy said.

For his part, Strickland admitted to temporarily losing his cool. "My emotions just got the best of me," he said. "I'm not too proud of that, but I can't take it back."

While the Giants' bullpen didn't get the job done in Game 2, the Royals got the opportunity to showcase their amazing bullpen to the World Series audience. The 1-2-3 punch of Kelvin Herrera, Wade Davis and Greg Holland tossed 3.2 innings of scoreless, one-hit relief to frustrate Giants hitters for the rest of the game. "Herrera is always on, and the more he gets out there, the better he is," said Holland after Herrera entered with two runners on base in the sixth but escaped unscathed to get Ventura off the hook. "Now we've got to win [four games] before they do."

	1	2	3	4	5	6	7	8	9	R	H	E
SAN FRANCISCO	1	0	0	1	0	0	0	0	0	2	9	0
KANSAS CITY	1	1	0	0	0	5	0	0	-	7	10	0

WP: Herrera LP: Peavy
HR: SF: Blanco KC: Infante

Blanco's homer in the first set the Giants up for early success, but the outfielder's line drive to deep right field would be one of just two runs scored.

Brandon Belt's RBI double in the fourth brought home third baseman Pablo Sandoval, who had reached base in his 25th straight postseason game.

"WE'VE BEEN IN DOGFIGHT AFTER DOGFIGHT THIS POSTSEASON AND LOST SOME HEARTBREAKERS. BUT WE'RE READY, AND WE'RE GOING TO GRIND IT OUT." *Jake Peavy*

Counterclockwise from top left: Infante capped off a five-run sixth inning with a homer off Strickland. One inning earlier, Sandoval knocked a two-base hit, his second of the Series. Mascot Sluggerrr celebrated the Royals' victory at The K before the Series moved back to San Francisco.

Tim Lincecum got his first taste of 2014 postseason play when he entered in relief in the seventh. He struck out two batters over 1.2 innings.

Right Off the Bat

THROUGH GAME 1 of this year's World Series, the San Francisco Giants had a perfect 5-0 record in postseason games in which they got on the board first. It looked like the trend would continue in Game 2, as leadoff batter Gregor Blanco, who began the season as the Giants' fourth outfielder, drilled a Yordano Ventura offering over the right-field wall to put the visitors ahead and seemingly set the tone for the game.

"[Blanco] had an incredible at-bat to lead off the game," said teammate Michael Morse. "He's finding every way to get on base, and that's what a good leadoff hitter does. He had a great approach and put us on the board early, and it felt good. We started right where we left off last night."

Blanco was also responsible for plating the Giants' first of seven runs a day earlier, as he led off Game 1 with a single and came around to score.

Overall, San Francisco got to Ventura and a trio of Kansas City relievers for nine hits in Game 2 — including Pablo Sandoval's 20th career postseason double — but was only able to translate those into two runs. The hometown boys, on the other hand, knocked 10 hits for seven runs, matching the Giants' run total from the previous evening.

GAME 3, OCT. 24

ROYALS 3, GIANTS 2

NOW THAT WAS more like it.

After two lopsided romps decided Games 1 and 2 in favor of the Giants and Royals, respectively, the World Series' third contest featured the tremendous defense and stellar bullpen work that had come to define these two teams throughout the season and the first three rounds of the playoffs.

"These teams have good pitching and defense," said the Giants' Gregor Blanco. "That's the way it should be."

After all, pitching and defense, as the saying goes, win games. When the contest opened, though, it seemed to have the potential to be another high-scoring affair, as Alcides Escobar started things off with a double off Giants starter Tim Hudson.

"I didn't think he was going to swing at the first pitch, but he did," Lorenzo Cain said. "He got things going. It was a great start to the first inning."

Two batters later, Cain grounded into a 6-3 fielder's choice that brought home Escobar.

Like in Game 2, the sixth inning was the charm for the offense, as both clubs put a pair of runs on the board. With two outs in the top of the frame, Manager Bruce Bochy brought in Javier Lopez to face first baseman Eric Hosmer. Hosmer celebrated his 25th birthday in style by fighting off 11 pitches to knock a two-out, RBI single, which scored what was ultimately the run that made the difference.

But it was what happened in the interim that was perhaps even more telling. In the second, Cain, who started the game in right field to accommodate Jarrod Dyson's first start in center, made a terrific sliding grab to rob Travis Ishikawa of a hit and end the inning. Giants right fielder Hunter Pence matched his counterpart's defensive display in the fourth, tracking down a long fly ball off the bat of none other than Cain himself, to help Hudson set the Royals down in order.

Both bullpens provided shutdown work from the sixth inning on, allowing no runs and just two hits combined. Third baseman Pablo Sandoval helped his relievers' efforts by making a great barehanded play on a soft dribbler from Hosmer, but the Royals managed to hang on when closer Greg Holland locked down the win with a 1-2-3 ninth inning.

	1	2	3	4	5	6	7	8	9	R	H	E
KANSAS CITY	1	0	0	0	0	2	0	0	0	3	6	0
SAN FRANCISCO	0	0	0	0	0	2	0	0	0	2	4	0

WP: Guthrie LP: Hudson
SV: Holland

With the Fall Classic tied at one game apiece, both teams arrived at San Francisco's AT&T Park looking to swing the Series in their favor.

Michael Morse contributed to the Giants' two-run sixth by launching a double to left field to bring home Brandon Crawford.

"YOU'D NEVER KNOW THERE'S PRESSURE. YOU LOOK AROUND THIS CLUBHOUSE, AND GUYS ARE SO PROFESSIONAL. THESE GUYS HAVE PLAYED IN SO MANY POSTSEASON GAMES, IT'S LIKE THEY HAVE ICE IN THEIR VEINS."

Michael Morse

"IT WAS GREAT BASEBALL TODAY. THIS IS WHAT WE EXPECTED IN THE FIRST TWO GAMES. WE'RE PRETTY EVENLY MATCHED, AND IT'S GOING TO BE A DOGFIGHT. WE PLAYED A GOOD BASEBALL GAME; THEY PLAYED A BETTER GAME. HOPEFULLY THINGS ARE REVERSED TOMORROW." *Jeremy Affeldt*

Spirited fans (left) donned Giants orange and black at AT&T Park. Shortstop Crawford scored on a double by teammate Morse in the sixth.

Joe Panik made his Major League debut in May and showed off his top-notch glovework at second base throughout the seven-game Series.

A Game in Hand

THE BACK END of the bullpen was front and center for both the Royals and Giants on their road to the Fall Classic. In addition to some characteristic clutch hits and stellar defense, both teams' relief corps shined again in Game 3. After the Royals took a 3-0 lead in the bottom of the sixth inning, the Giants opened the frame with two straight hits to chase starter Jeremy Guthrie. But that's when Kansas City Manager Ned Yost signaled for Kelvin Herrera, and the Royals relievers took over. A group that finished Game 3 with a perfect 7-0 record and 1.66 ERA in the 2014 postseason tossed four more scoreless innings, as Brandon Finnegan, Wade Davis and Greg Holland followed Herrera.

"Our bullpen has been monstrous," Yost said. "Probably the key factors in all of this for us are timely hitting, great defense, really solid starting pitching and that dynamic back of the bullpen."

The San Francisco bullpen had another great night as well, posting 3.1 innings of scoreless relief to keep the game tight. Through Game 3, Giants relievers had posted a 2.06 ERA over 43.2 innings this postseason.

"I thought our 'pen did a great job," Giants Manager Bruce Bochy said. "That's a good, tight ballgame, and both sides pitched well. They pitched a little better than we did, and that was the difference in the game."

In a tight race for the title, both bullpens continued to provide dramatic action as the Series stretched on.

GAME 4, OCT. 25

GIANTS 11, ROYALS 4

STARING A POTENTIAL 3-games-to-1 Series deficit in the face, the Giants' bats finally exploded in Game 4. The Royals led, 4-1, in the third inning, but instead of buckling, San Francisco came alive to pound starter Jason Vargas and a trio of middle relievers, denying Kansas City the chance to turn over the game to its bullpen. "We were able to get it done before those [Big Three] relievers came around, but we weren't worried about who we were facing," said Giants leadoff man Gregor Blanco, who went 2 for 5 and scored three runs.

Hunter Pence led the hit parade, going 3 for 5 with a double, three RBI and two runs scored, which raised his World Series batting average to .467 through the first four games. "It's not just the hits; Hunter brings a lot of energy out there," said teammate Buster Posey.

Chasing Vargas from the game early became key for the Giants. They were just 1 for their first 17 against Kansas City relievers with runners in scoring position in the World Series. But when Pence faced righty reliever Jason Frasor in the fifth, he laced an RBI single to cut the Royals' lead to 4-3. From there, Giants hitters caught fire, going 6 for their next 12 and ripping open the game with two runs in the fifth inning, three in the sixth and four in the seventh to grab a commanding 11-4 lead that they wouldn't relinquish. The top five hitters in their lineup tallied 10 hits, and every starting position player collected at least one, including two more hits and as many RBI from 23-year-old rookie second baseman Joe Panik. "He has been doing that ever since he came up [from the Minors]," double play partner Brandon Crawford said. "Nothing is too big for him."

After all the talk about the Royals' bullpen, Giants relievers again showed what they're made of, tossing 6.1 scoreless innings, including three from Yusmeiro Petit to earn the victory. That iced Game 4 and guaranteed that the Series would return to Kansas City and last at least six games. "We never give up," said Pablo Sandoval, who went 2 for 5 with two RBI in the rout. "They could put [the Big Three] in, and we'll do our best against anybody. We have a great bullpen, too."

	1	2	3	4	5	6	7	8	9	R	H	E
KANSAS CITY	0	0	4	0	0	0	0	0	0	4	12	1
SAN FRANCISCO	1	0	1	0	2	3	4	0	-	11	16	0

WP: Petit LP: Finnegan

Blanco started things off with a walk before scoring the Giants' initial run in the first inning.

Pence had a standout night, lacing an RBI single in the fifth, followed by an RBI double two innings later.

"IT WAS A NICE EFFORT ALL THE WAY AROUND. WE PUT PRESSURE ON THEM, LAID DOWN BUNTS AND WERE ABLE TO COME THROUGH WITH RUNNERS IN SCORING POSITION." *Buster Posey*

Michael Morse (far left) and Blanco combined for four runs in Game 4. Posey (above left) and Hunter Strickland celebrated their club's performance.

A GIANT OUTBURST

IT'S NOT AS if the Giants' bats had been quiet early on. Through Game 3, San Francisco had collected 24 World Series hits and converted them into 11 runs, but the club trailed Kansas City, 2 games to 1, on the eve of Game 4. That contest had the potential to change the tide of the Series: The Giants could tie it with one more to play at home, or the Royals could go up by two with the potential for a Game 5 clinch.

The hometown team left nothing to chance. Gregor Blanco drew a walk to open the home half of the first, reaching base in his first at-bat for the third time in the Series' first four games. The Giants' lineup soon erupted, as 11 different players collected at least one hit in the 11-4 rout, setting a record for a National League team in the World Series. The total also matched the all-time World Series record, held by the 1928 and 1960 Yankees.

"It's huge that everyone is contributing," said Brandon Belt, who collected an RBI single in the sixth.

The top of the lineup was especially potent, as Blanco, Joe Panik, Buster Posey, Hunter Pence and Pablo Sandoval combined for 10 of San Francisco's 16 hits on the night.

"PABLO LIVES FOR MOMENTS LIKE THESE. WHEN YOU NEED HIM MOST, THAT'S WHEN HE'S BEST." *Brandon Belt*

Sandoval kept up the game's momentum, blasting a go-ahead single off Kansas City reliever Brandon Finnegan in the bottom of the sixth.

GAME 5, OCT. 26

GIANTS 5, ROYALS 0

FROM THE OUTSET, Game 5 was San Francisco's for the taking. Riding the momentum of a seven-run victory from the previous night, the home team had ace Madison Bumgarner on the mound in front of a crowd that stayed on its feet since the pregame festivities featuring Billy Crystal and the children of the late Robin Williams got them going.

It was clear early on that the left-hander was dealing, and his performance didn't waver. "[Bumgarner] cruised," said batterymate Buster Posey. "He was really strong even in the ninth inning. His fastball had a lot of life. With the amount of innings he had on his arm, it's incredible to be that sharp."

The 25-year-old tallied 47.2 postseason innings through Game 5, the second-highest total ever and the most by a left-hander. Showing no signs of slowing down, he silenced Royals batters throughout his complete-game shutout. He held their lineup to just four hits and didn't allow a runner to advance past second base.

"Bum is so tough," said Kansas City's Alcides Escobar. "It's unbelievable."

The Giants' bats were slow to help Bumgarner's cause early on, but they managed to scratch a few runs across the board. Shortstop Brandon Crawford was responsible for their tallies in both the second and the fourth, via a 4-3 fielder's choice that plated Hunter Pence and a line drive

single to score Pablo Sandoval. The final three runs didn't come until the bottom of the eighth, when Crawford again knocked an RBI single after Juan Perez nearly took reliever Wade Davis deep, doubling off the center-field wall.

"It was an emotional night all the way around," said Perez, who found out about the death of the Cardinals' Oscar Taveras, his close friend and NLCS foe, during the game. "But we have to go out and do our job on the field."

Untold in the lopsided final score was the impressive six-inning outing from Royals starter James Shields, who was accountable for the first two runs yet got zero help on offense. Omar Infante represented the lone threat in scoring position, knocking a double in the top of the fifth.

Heading back to Kansas City, the Giants were in position to clinch their third title on the road in five years. Back in 2010, the San Francisco squad defeated the Rangers in Game 5 in Arlington, and the 2012 Series ended with a Game 4 clinch in Detroit.

"We want to try to finish it [in Game 6]," Sandoval said.

	1	2	3	4	5	6	7	8	9	R	H	E
KANSAS CITY	0	0	0	0	0	0	0	0	0	0	4	1
SAN FRANCISCO	0	1	0	1	0	0	0	3	-	5	12	0

WP: Bumgarner LP: Shields

Above, the children of late actor Robin Williams, who was a devout Giants fan, partook in pregame festivities in front of a roaring San Francisco crowd.

The duo of Pence (left) and Sandoval combined for four hits and four runs to support Bumgarner's complete-game shutout.

"[BUMGARNER] DIDN'T LOOK LIKE HE WAS RUNNING OUT OF GAS, THAT'S FOR SURE. WE DIDN'T HAVE TO USE ANY OF OUR BULLPEN, EITHER, SO THAT WAS HUGE."

Brandon Crawford

San Francisco ace Bumgarner made history during Game 5 when he tossed the first World Series shutout since 2003.

ALL-TIME BUM

KOUFAX. GIBSON. BUMGARNER. After another utterly masterful start in Game 5, Giants 25-year-old southpaw Madison Bumgarner cemented his name as one of the most dominant starting pitchers in World Series history. In fact, among hurlers with at least 25 career innings pitched, MadBum's 0.25 ERA ranks as the best of all time, just ahead of Jack Billingham (0.36) of the mid-1970s Reds. Sandy Koufax threw 24 innings with the Dodgers in the 1965 Fall Classic while recording a 0.38 ERA, and Cardinals legend Bob Gibson, who pitched 27 innings each during three Series in the '60s, posted a 1.00 ERA at his best in the 1967 contest.

Bumgarner also became just the fourth pitcher to throw multiple shutouts in the same postseason, joining Orel Hershiser, Randy Johnson and Josh Beckett. "It's very humbling to have an opportunity to do that," Bumgarner said. "That's surprising. I wouldn't have thought that."

Royals hitters felt humbled in Game 5, as well. Bumgarner surrendered just four hits in the complete-game shutout, and allowed just one runner to advance to second base.

"He was pumping first-pitch strikes," said Royals slugger Billy Butler, who pinch-hit in the eighth and was called out on strikes following a devastating breaking ball. "He had a great game today."

Adding to his legend with each pitch, Bumgarner also became the first hurler in Fall Classic history to toss a shutout with no walks and at least eight strikeouts. "When you get this guy on, it's fun to watch," said Giants Manager Bruce Bochy. "He was hitting his spots and had great stuff. I just felt like it was his game."

"GOING INTO KANSAS CITY UP 3-2 IS A POSITIVE. BUT I CAN TELL YOU, THEY'RE NOT GOING TO MAKE IT EASY. WE'VE GOT TO WIN FOUR GAMES TO WIN THE WORLD SERIES, AND WE HAVEN'T DONE THAT YET." *Jeremy Affeldt*

Crawford kicked off a three-RBI night in the second when he drove in Pence on a groundout. Two innings later, he singled to bring home Sandoval.

GAME 6, OCT. 28

ROYALS 10, GIANTS 0

THE ROYALS RETURNED to Kauffman Stadium with high hopes of erasing the memory of their losses in the last two games in San Francisco to put themselves in a 3-games-to-2 hole. They wasted no time roughing up Giants starter Jake Peavy in Game 6, firmly proving that their magical ride through the postseason wasn't over yet. "It's great to bring this Series home to this crowd and get them behind us," said outfielder Lorenzo Cain, who went 2 for 3 and reached base four times. "I'm just excited to be part of this team."

Kansas City batted around in the bottom of the second inning, plating seven runs to get The K rocking. Eight players got hits in the inning, including doubles from Billy Butler and Mike Moustakas; and five different players drove in runs, including a two-run single from Cain. If his offensive contributions weren't enough, the outfielder made yet another spectacular running catch to rob Joe Panik of extra bases in the first inning. "He's a huge part of why we're here," Moustakas said of Cain. "He's done this all year. The way he grinds it out is awesome to watch."

In addition to Cain, five other Royals collected two base knocks in the 15-hit barrage: Alcides Escobar, Eric Hosmer, Salvador Perez, Mike Moustakas and Omar Infante. The attack was balanced, but the Nos. 7–9 hitters, Perez, Moustakas and Infante, combined to go 6 for 12 with five runs scored. "They've been a part of win or go home, as well," said the Giants' Hunter Pence. "Tonight was their night."

On the hill, Royals starter Yordano Ventura was at his best, totally shutting down the Giants' offense. The 23-year-old fireballer allowed just three hits in seven innings of much needed domination. "It's incredible to see a guy that young stay unfazed," teammate Greg Holland said. "He's not affected by situations. He's just out there like he's the best pitcher on the planet, and that's a huge reason we're here."

Ventura started off the game with a strikeout of Gregor Blanco, and, as his team faced the pressure of elimination, he stayed in complete control, with the exception of walking the bases loaded in the third inning before getting a 6-3 double play. "He's not scared when he goes out there," Escobar said of Ventura. "He just says, 'I like situations like these.'"

The 10-0 rout guaranteed just the second World Series Game 7 since the Giants lost to the Angels in 2002, and the first winner-take-all matchup since 2011. "We want to leave it all out there [in Game 7]," Hosmer said. "In that spot, you're where you've spent you're whole life wanting to be."

	1	2	3	4	5	6	7	8	9	R	H	E
SAN FRANCISCO	0	0	0	0	0	0	0	0	0	0	6	0
KANSAS CITY	0	7	1	0	1	0	1	0	-	10	15	0

WP: Ventura LP: Peavy

Veteran hurler Ryan Vogelsong (left) entered in the eighth to keep the Royals' bats at bay, while Pablo Sandoval made play after play at third.

Pence's double in the second marked his 10th knock of the Series, but the Giants couldn't convert the outfielder's hit, or any others that night, into a run.

"GAME 7 OF THE WORLD SERIES IS A GIFT FOR EVERYONE. IT'S INCREDIBLY ENTERTAINING FOR THE WORLD. ONCE A GAME IS OVER, WIN, LOSE OR DRAW, YOU LET IT GO AND MOVE ONTO THE NEXT ONE. WHAT'S IN FRONT OF US IS A GAME 7 OPPORTUNITY." *Hunter Pence*

"STATISTICS ARE ALWAYS CHANGING. YOU CAN'T LOOK AT THE PAST. AFTER A 10-0 LOSS, YOU WANT TO MOVE FORWARD. TOMORROW'S ANOTHER DAY. THE MOMENTUM GOES BACK AND FORTH." *Joe Panik*

While Sergio Romo (far right) didn't pitch in the game, his bullpen mates threw a combined 6.2 frames of relief in the Giants' loss.

Rookie hurler Ventura and the Royals returned to Kansas City for Game 6, where he picked up his first postseason win.

Going the Distance

WITH THEIR BACKS against the wall, the Royals headed home to Kansas City facing a do-or-die Game 6. But they showed they would come out fighting, jumping on Giants starter Jake Peavy and scoring seven runs on eight hits as they batted around in the second inning.

The result, a 10-0 drubbing of San Francisco — in which the entire lineup had recorded at least one hit by the end of the third inning for just the second time in history — marked the fifth lopsided affair of the 2014 World Series. Through Game 6, every contest except Game 3 was decided by five or more runs, the first time that has ever happened. "To put up runs in a flurry like [in the second inning], it makes you confident," third baseman Mike Moustakas said. "The best part, though, is that we didn't stop there. We kept adding on."

Despite the mismatched individual results throughout the Fall Classic, the Series was knotted at three games apiece following Game 6. Both the Giants and Royals were placed on notice heading into the first Game 7 matchup since 2011.

"By the end of the game, whoever the winner is, is going to say that it was a hard-fought battle," said Giants reliever Jeremy Affeldt, who owns rings with both the 2010 and '12 Giants. "When you have a Game 7, it was an earned championship."

GAME 7, OCT. 29

GIANTS 3, ROYALS 2

DRAMA LIKE THIS was only fitting.

Just five games earlier, which, frankly, seemed like an eternity ago in the first Series to go seven games since 2011, Hunter Pence declared that stakes this high were exciting. "The more games you play, the more intense it gets," said the two-time world champion. "Drama is good for this game."

It wasn't until the bottom of the ninth inning, though, that the contest had a true Game 7 feel. With two outs and Giants ace Madison Bumgarner on the mound in his fifth inning of relief on just two days' rest, Alex Gordon got the home crowd going with a single to center field, which he stretched into a three-bagger after Gregor Blanco let the ball past him. "I was starting to get a little nervous," Bumgarner admitted. "[Gordon] can run, and it's a big outfield. I just wanted someone to get it in."

But Bum quelled the threat and shut the door, getting the next batter, Salvador Perez, to pop out to third baseman Pablo Sandoval in foul territory. "You know they're an aggressive team," said the 25-year-old, who set numerous Fall Classic records and earned the save to top it off. "We tried to use that aggressiveness against them and throw up in the zone, a little bit higher than high."

Sandoval, who collapsed to the ground in euphoria after nabbing the final out in foul territory, also came up big at the plate, reaching base four times and scoring twice to wrap up the Series with a .429 average.

After getting on the board first for the fifth time this Series, San Francisco got help on defense from Joe Panik. In the bottom of the third, the middle infielder dove to snare an Eric Hosmer grounder up the middle, and then flipped the ball from his glove to shortstop Brandon Crawford for the double play. Hosmer was originally called safe at first, but Manager Bruce Bochy challenged and the call was overturned. The play reversal dramatically altered the situation from one with runners on first and second with no outs, to one with no runners on and two down.

"It's the first time I've ever done something like that," said Panik, who experienced an abundance of firsts in his freshman campaign.

The momentum from Panik's defensive gem carried over into the bottom half of the frame, when DH Michael Morse laced an RBI single, plating the run that would provide the ultimate margin of victory.

"It still hasn't set in," said a champagne-soaked Panik. "I just wish we could have scored a couple more runs to make it a little bit easier."

	1	2	3	4	5	6	7	8	9	R	H	E
SAN FRANCISCO	0	2	0	1	0	0	0	0	0	3	8	1
KANSAS CITY	0	2	0	0	0	0	0	0	0	2	6	0

WP: Affeldt LP: Guthrie
SV: Bumgarner

Panik's back-handed gem (left) kept the Giants off the bases in the third, while Sandoval's 26 hits in the 2014 postseason set an MLB record.

Bumgarner finished the Series with two wins and a save. He received MVP honors for his performance, which included a 0.43 ERA over 21 innings.

"YOU ALWAYS HAVE CONFIDENCE IN BUM, BUT THERE WERE STILL A LOT OF INNINGS TO BE PLAYED [WHEN HE CAME IN]. HE'S OUR GUY. ONCE HE HAD THAT BALL IN THE FIFTH INNING, NOBODY ELSE WAS COMING IN."

Hunter Pence

"I REALLY BELIEVE THAT [YOU'RE GOING TO BE HARD-PRESSED TO FIND ANOTHER POSTSEASON PERFORMANCE] LIKE THAT. IF YOU DO, IT WON'T BE FOR A LONG TIME."

Buster Posey

Pence (center) showered his teammates with champagne and led them in a "Yes! Yes! Yes!" chant after they won their eighth world title in franchise history.

San Francisco celebrated at The K after Bumgarner recorded his third dominant outing of the Series.

A Mad, Mad World

UTTER DOMINATION. AFTER Madison Bumgarner shut out Kansas City in Game 5 to give the Giants a 3-games-to-2 Series advantage, you couldn't blame the Royals for hoping they had seen the last of him. But with the Giants clinging to a 3-2 lead in the fifth inning of Game 7, the bullpen door opened and MadBum emerged, much to Kansas City's dismay.

"I never felt like it was over, especially with that team," Brandon Belt said of the never-say-die Royals. "But I have a lot of confidence when [Bumgarner] comes in."

Bumgarner warranted that confidence, as he fired five more scoreless innings in relief to earn the save and take home the Fall Classic MVP Award after already capturing NLCS MVP honors. He finished the World Series with a 2-0 record, 17 strikeouts and a 0.43 ERA, the lowest single-Series mark since Sandy Koufax's 0.38 in 1965.

"He was the difference maker for them," said Royals DH Billy Butler. "He put the team on his back and carried them."

In his three career World Series, Bumgarner has maintained a microscopic 0.25 ERA, which ranks as the best ever with a minimum of 25 innings pitched, so it's no wonder Giants Manager Bruce Bochy gave him the ball one last time in Game 7.

"I wasn't thinking about when I'd get in or the number of pitches," Bumgarner said. "I was just thinking about getting outs, and we were able to do that for the most part."

Still in awe after the Giants' win, Royals first baseman Eric Hosmer reflected on his opponent's dominance: "For a guy who pitched two days ago, to come back and throw like that is impressive."

The big lefty's 52.2 innings pitched in the 2014 postseason also set a record, surpassing Curt Schilling's 48.1 frames in 2001, and it lowered his career postseason ERA to 1.03, good for third-best ever among hurlers with a minimum of 30 innings pitched.

And after all those October innings, Bum finally laughed and let reporters in on a secret once it was all over: "You know, I can't lie to you anymore; I'm a little tired."

POSTSEASON STATS

NO.	PLAYER	W	L	ERA	SO	BB	SV
PITCHERS							
41	Jeremy Affeldt	2	0	0.00	2	2	0
40	Madison Bumgarner	4	1	1.03	45	6	1
46	Santiago Casilla	0	0	0.00	7	3	4
17	Tim Hudson	0	1	4.29	16	2	0
55	Tim Lincecum	0	0	0.00	2	0	0
49	Javier Lopez	0	0	0.00	4	1	0
63	Jean Machi	0	0	7.94	4	2	0
22	Jake Peavy	1	2	6.19	8	9	0
52	Yusmeiro Petit	3	0	1.42	13	4	0
54	Sergio Romo	1	1	1.29	7	0	0
60	Hunter Strickland	1	0	7.56	8	2	1
32	Ryan Vogelsong	0	0	6.57	8	6	0

NO.	PLAYER	AB	H	AVG	HR	RBI	OBP
CATCHERS							
28	Buster Posey	69	17	.246	0	7	.312
34	Andrew Susac	4	1	.250	0	0	.250
INFIELDERS							
13	Joaquin Arias	4	2	.500	0	1	.500
9	Brandon Belt	61	18	.295	1	8	.397
35	Brandon Crawford	61	15	.246	1	9	.314
50	Matt Duffy	6	1	.167	0	0	.167
45	Travis Ishikawa	39	10	.256	1	7	.326
12	Joe Panik	73	17	.233	1	8	.273
48	Pablo Sandoval	71	26	.366	0	5	.423
OUTFIELDERS							
7	Gregor Blanco	72	11	.153	1	5	.256
56	Gary Brown	1	0	.000	0	0	.000
38	Michael Morse	20	6	.300	1	5	.318
8	Hunter Pence	66	22	.333	1	8	.405
2	Juan Perez	25	5	.200	0	3	.250

SAN FRANCISCO GIANTS POSTSEASON HISTORY

M^cNALLY STEALS HOME   SS 60-11

Baseball's New York Giants called the Polo Grounds home from 1891–1957, hosting 14 of the club's World Series appearances at the stadium.

1905*
WORLD SERIES

GIANTS 4, PHILADELPHIA ATHLETICS 1
Oct. 9 Giants 3 at Athletics 0
Oct. 10 Athletics 3 at Giants 0
Oct. 12 Giants 9 at Athletics 0
Oct. 13 Athletics 0 at Giants 1
Oct. 14 Athletics 0 at Giants 2

THE 1905 GIANTS finished the season with a 105-48 record behind a dominant pitching staff led by 25-year-old Christy Mathewson. They took on the 92-win A's in the World Series, during which the Hall-of-Fame pitcher turned in three gems that collectively rank among one of the greatest Fall Classic pitching performances in history. The right-hander began the Series against the A's with a four-hit shutout in Game 1, a result he replicated in Game 3. Pitching on just one day's rest in Game 5, Mathewson hurled his third complete-game shutout, which still stands as an all-time Fall Classic record, to give the Giants their first title.

1911
WORLD SERIES

PHILADELPHIA ATHLETICS 4, GIANTS 2
Oct. 14 Athletics 1 at Giants 2
Oct. 16 Giants 1 at Athletics 3
Oct. 17 Athletics 3 at Giants 2
Oct. 24 Giants 2 at Athletics 4
Oct. 25 Athletics 3 at Giants 4
Oct. 26 Giants 2 at Athletics 13

1912
WORLD SERIES

BOSTON RED SOX 4, GIANTS 3
Oct. 8 Red Sox 4 at Giants 3
Oct. 9 Giants 6 at Red Sox 6
Oct. 10 Giants 2 at Red Sox 1
Oct. 11 Red Sox 3 at Giants 1
Oct. 12 Giants 1 at Red Sox 2
Oct. 14 Red Sox 2 at Giants 5
Oct. 15 Giants 11 at Red Sox 4
Oct. 16 Giants 2 at Red Sox 3

1913
WORLD SERIES

PHILADELPHIA ATHLETICS 4, GIANTS 1
Oct. 7 Athletics 6 at Giants 4
Oct. 8 Giants 3 at Athletics 0
Oct. 9 Athletics 8 at Giants 2
Oct. 10 Giants 5 at Athletics 6
Oct. 11 Athletics 3 at Giants 1

1917
WORLD SERIES

CHICAGO WHITE SOX 4, GIANTS 2
Oct. 6 Giants 1 at White Sox 2
Oct. 7 Giants 2 at White Sox 7
Oct. 10 White Sox 0 at Giants 2
Oct. 11 White Sox 0 at Giants 5
Oct. 13 Giants 5 at White Sox 8
Oct. 15 White Sox 4 at Giants 2

1921*
WORLD SERIES

GIANTS 5, NEW YORK YANKEES 3
Oct. 5 Yankees 3 at Giants 0
Oct. 6 Giants 0 at Yankees 3
Oct. 7 Yankees 5 at Giants 13
Oct. 9 Giants 4 at Yankees 2
Oct. 10 Yankees 3 at Giants 1
Oct. 11 Giants 8 at Yankees 5
Oct. 12 Yankees 1 at Giants 2
Oct. 13 Giants 1 at Yankees 0

IN THE 1910s, the Giants failed to translate their decade-long success into a championship, with four

Over four Series with the Giants, Mathewson owned a 0.97 ERA.

* Giants World Series victory

83

teams losing the World Series after posting 98-plus victories during the regular season. In 1921, the franchise finally snapped that streak, beating the Babe Ruth–led Yankees in the first Subway Series and last best-of-nine Series in Fall Classic history. Behind an offense bolstered by first baseman "High Pockets" Kelly, the Giants led the league in runs, but used strong pitching to close out their crosstown rivals in eight games. Twenty-game winner Art Nehf capped the victory by pitching a complete-game shutout in the clinching game. All eight contests were played at the Polo Grounds — the first time in history that each World Series game was played at the same site.

1922*
WORLD SERIES

GIANTS 4, NEW YORK YANKEES 0
Oct. 4 Yankees 2 at Giants 3
Oct. 5 Giants 3 at Yankees 3
Oct. 6 Yankees 0 at Giants 3
Oct. 7 Giants 4 at Yankees 3
Oct. 8 Yankees 3 at Giants 5

THE REMATCH OF the prior year's World Series finished with a clean sweep, but it was not without controversy. The thrilling Game 2 ended in a tie after 10 innings when the umpires inexplicably called it, citing darkness even though it was only 4:45 p.m. It was the third and final tie game in Fall Classic history. A near-riot ensued among the 37,000 fans at the Polo Grounds, with customers demanding their money back. When play resumed the following day, the Giants took command. Their offensive star, outfielder Irish Meusel, drove in seven runs in the Series after collecting 132 RBI during the regular season. The Giants scored three in the bottom of the eighth inning in Game 5, as Art Nehf once again sealed the championship with a complete-game win.

1923
WORLD SERIES

NEW YORK YANKEES 4, GIANTS 2
Oct. 10 Giants 5 at Yankees 4
Oct. 11 Yankees 4 at Giants 2
Oct. 12 Giants 1 at Yankees 0
Oct. 13 Yankees 8 at Giants 4
Oct. 14 Giants 1 at Yankees 8
Oct. 15 Yankees 6 at Giants 4

Ott boasted two homers and four RBI in the 1933 Fall Classic.

1924
WORLD SERIES

WASHINGTON SENATORS 4, GIANTS 3
Oct. 4 Giants 4 at Senators 3
Oct. 5 Giants 3 at Senators 4
Oct. 6 Senators 4 at Giants 6
Oct. 7 Senators 7 at Giants 4
Oct. 8 Senators 2 at Giants 6
Oct. 9 Giants 1 at Senators 2
Oct. 10 Giants 3 at Senators 4

1933*
WORLD SERIES

GIANTS 4, WASHINGTON SENATORS 1
Oct. 3 Senators 2 at Giants 4
Oct. 4 Senators 1 at Giants 6
Oct. 5 Giants 0 at Senators 4
Oct. 6 Giants 2 at Senators 1
Oct. 7 Giants 4 at Senators 3

THE 1933 SEASON was the first without Manager John McGraw at the helm since 1901. The legendary skipper retired with 2,763 career wins — a record total that would eventually be surpassed by Connie Mack — and 10 pennants. First baseman Bill Terry took over as a player-manager, while Hall of Famer Mel Ott carried the offensive load and Carl Hubbell dominated on the mound in both the regular season and the World Series. Ott knocked seven hits, including two homers, in 18 Fall Classic at-bats, while Hubbell won Games 1 and 4, tossing a combined 20 innings and allowing just 13 hits. An extra-inning victory at Griffith Stadium in Game 5 ended the 99-win Senators' surprising season.

1936
WORLD SERIES
NEW YORK YANKEES 4, GIANTS 2
Sept. 30 Yankees 1 at Giants 6
Oct. 2 Yankees 18 at Giants 4
Oct. 3 Giants 1 at Yankees 2
Oct. 4 Giants 2 at Yankees 5
Oct. 5 Giants 5 at Yankees 4
Oct. 6 Yankees 13 at Giants 5

1937
WORLD SERIES
NEW YORK YANKEES 4, GIANTS 1
Oct. 6 Giants 1 at Yankees 8
Oct. 7 Giants 1 at Yankees 8
Oct. 8 Yankees 5 at Giants 1
Oct. 9 Yankees 3 at Giants 7
Oct. 10 Yankees 4 at Giants 2

1951
WORLD SERIES
NEW YORK YANKEES 4, GIANTS 2
Oct. 4 Giants 5 at Yankees 1
Oct. 5 Giants 1 at Yankees 3
Oct. 6 Yankees 2 at Giants 6
Oct. 8 Yankees 6 at Giants 2
Oct. 9 Yankees 13 at Giants 1
Oct. 10 Giants 3 at Yankees 4

1954*
WORLD SERIES
GIANTS 4, CLEVELAND INDIANS 0
Sept. 29 Indians 2 at Giants 5
Sept. 30 Indians 1 at Giants 3
Oct. 1 Giants 6 at Indians 2
Oct. 2 Giants 7 at Indians 4

EVEN FANS WHO did not attend Game 1 of the 1954 World Series at the Polo Grounds are familiar with the

image of Willie Mays racing to deep center field, some 415 feet from home plate, and corralling the ball over his left shoulder to rob Cleveland's Vic Wertz of a sure extra-base hit. "The Catch" preserved a tie in the eighth inning and set the tone for the remainder of the Series. New York never looked back after that game, finishing off the favored Indians, who had won an incredible 111 games during the regular season, in just four games. Little-known outfielder Dusty Rhodes came up with several clutch pinch-hits, including the game-winning roundtripper in the 10th inning of Game 1, to key the Giants' triumph.

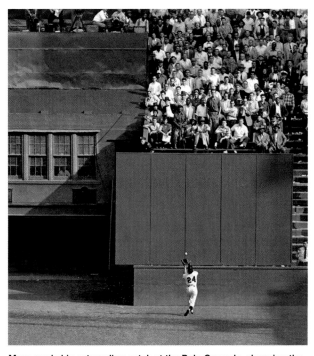

Mays made his astounding catch at the Polo Grounds, changing the course of the game and supporting the Giants' win over the Indians in Game 1 of the 1954 Fall Classic.

1962
WORLD SERIES
NEW YORK YANKEES 4, GIANTS 3
Oct. 4 Yankees 6 at Giants 2
Oct. 5 Yankees 0 at Giants 2
Oct. 7 Giants 2 at Yankees 3
Oct. 8 Giants 7 at Yankees 3
Oct. 10 Giants 3 at Yankees 5
Oct. 15 Yankees 2 at Giants 5
Oct. 16 Yankees 1 at Giants 0

Lincecum earned two of the Giants' four wins in the 2010 World Series. The Freak pitched 13.2 innings with 13 strikeouts against the Rangers.

1971
NLCS

PITTSBURGH PIRATES 3, GIANTS 1
Oct. 2 Pirates 4 at Giants 5
Oct. 3 Pirates 9 at Giants 4
Oct. 5 Giants 1 at Pirates 2
Oct. 6 Giants 5 at Pirates 9

1987
NLCS

ST. LOUIS CARDINALS 4, GIANTS 3
Oct. 6 Giants 3 at Cardinals 5
Oct. 7 Giants 5 at Cardinals 0
Oct. 9 Cardinals 6 at Giants 5
Oct. 10 Cardinals 2 at Giants 4
Oct. 11 Cardinals 3 at Giants 6
Oct. 13 Giants 0 at Cardinals 1
Oct. 14 Giants 0 at Cardinals 6

1989
NLCS

GIANTS 4, CHICAGO CUBS 1
Oct. 4 Giants 11 at Cubs 3
Oct. 5 Giants 5 at Cubs 9
Oct. 7 Cubs 4 at Giants 5
Oct. 8 Cubs 4 at Giants 6
Oct. 9 Cubs 2 at Giants 3

WORLD SERIES

OAKLAND ATHLETICS 4, GIANTS 0
Oct. 14 Giants 0 at Athletics 5
Oct. 15 Giants 1 at Athletics 5
Oct. 27 Athletics 13 at Giants 7
Oct. 28 Athletics 9 at Giants 6

1997
NLDS

FLORIDA MARLINS 3, GIANTS 0
Sept. 30 Giants 1 at Marlins 2
Oct. 1 Giants 6 at Marlins 7
Oct. 3 Marlins 6 at Giants 2

2000
NLDS

NEW YORK METS 3, GIANTS 1
Oct. 4 Mets 1 at Giants 5
Oct. 5 Mets 5 at Giants 4
Oct. 7 Giants 2 at Mets 3
Oct. 8 Giants 0 at Mets 4

2002
NLDS

GIANTS 3, ATLANTA BRAVES 2
Oct. 2 Giants 8 at Braves 5
Oct. 3 Giants 3 at Braves 7
Oct. 5 Braves 10 at Giants 2
Oct. 6 Braves 3 at Giants 8
Oct. 7 Giants 3 at Braves 1

NLCS

GIANTS 4, ST. LOUIS CARDINALS 1
Oct. 9 Giants 9 at Cardinals 6
Oct. 10 Giants 4 at Cardinals 1
Oct. 12 Cardinals 5 at Giants 4
Oct. 13 Cardinals 3 at Giants 4
Oct. 14 Cardinals 1 at Giants 2

WORLD SERIES

ANAHEIM ANGELS 4, GIANTS 3
Oct. 19 Giants 4 at Angels 3
Oct. 20 Giants 10 at Angels 11
Oct. 22 Angels 10 at Giants 4
Oct. 23 Angels 3 at Giants 4
Oct. 24 Angels 4 at Giants 16

Oct. 26 Giants 5 at Angels 6
Oct. 27 Giants 1 at Angels 4

2003
NLDS
FLORIDA MARLINS 3, GIANTS 1
Sept. 30 Marlins 0 at Giants 2
Oct. 1 Marlins 9 at Giants 5
Oct. 3 Giants 3 at Marlins 4
Oct. 4 Giants 6 at Marlins 7

2010*
NLDS
GIANTS 3, ATLANTA BRAVES 1
Oct. 7 Braves 0 at Giants 1
Oct. 8 Braves 5 at Giants 4
Oct. 10 Giants 3 at Braves 2
Oct. 11 Giants 3 at Braves 2

NLCS
GIANTS 4, PHILADELPHIA PHILLIES 2
Oct. 16 Giants 4 at Phillies 3
Oct. 17 Giants 1 at Phillies 6
Oct. 19 Phillies 0 at Giants 3
Oct. 20 Phillies 5 at Giants 6
Oct 21 Phillies 4 at Giants 2
Oct. 23 Giants 3 at Phillies 2

WORLD SERIES
GIANTS 4, TEXAS RANGERS 1
Oct. 27 Rangers 7 at Giants 11
Oct. 28 Rangers 0 at Giants 9
Oct. 30 Giants 2 at Rangers 4
Oct. 31 Giants 4 at Rangers 0
Nov. 1 Giants 3 at Rangers 1

OF ALL THE terrific memories the Giants had given the San Francisco faithful in their first five decades since relocating to the West Coast, a World Series was not one of them. In 2010, that changed. The ragtag Giants made history, becoming San Francisco's first champions of the baseball world.

Manager Bruce Bochy affectionately referred to his team as a bunch of "castoffs and misfits," but it was those same castoffs and misfits who steamrolled through the playoffs, eventually beating the offensive goliath Texas Rangers in just five games to win the Fall Classic.

A powerful rotation led by Tim Lincecum, a strong bullpen anchored by Brian Wilson, and a scrappy lineup that could hit in the clutch fired on all cylinders at precisely the right time, conjuring up Bay Area baseball magic in October.

2012*
NLDS
GIANTS 3, CINCINNATI REDS 2
Oct. 6 Reds 5 at Giants 2
Oct. 7 Reds 9 at Giants 0
Oct. 9 Giants 2 at Reds 1
Oct. 10 Giants 8 at Reds 3
Oct. 11 Giants 6 at Reds 4

NLCS
GIANTS 4, ST. LOUIS CARDINALS 3
Oct. 14 Cardinals 6 at Giants 4
Oct. 15 Cardinals 1 at Giants 7
Oct. 17 Giants 1 at Cardinals 3
Oct. 18 Giants 3 at Cardinals 8
Oct. 19 Giants 5 at Cardinals 0
Oct. 21 Cardinals 1 at Giants 6
Oct. 22 Cardinals 0 at Giants 9

WORLD SERIES
GIANTS 4, DETROIT TIGERS 0
Oct. 24 Tigers 3 at Giants 8
Oct. 25 Tigers 0 at Giants 2
Oct. 27 Giants 2 at Tigers 0
Oct. 28 Giants 4 at Tigers 3

AFTER CAPTURING THE championship in 2010, San Francisco failed to even make the playoffs in 2011, finishing in second place in the NL West. But the Giants didn't stay down for long. San Francisco won the division crown in 2012, and its first two postseason series went the distance, as the club won six consecutive elimination games to get a shot at the Fall Classic.

The World Series came much easier. In Game 1, eventual Series MVP Pablo Sandoval tied a Fall Classic record with three home runs in one game, contributing to an 8-3 win. Pitching dominated the next three contests, as San Francisco won all three without scoring more than four runs in any game, including two shutouts of Detroit, en route to the franchise's second championship in three years.

Giants World Series victory

INSIDE THE WORLD SERIES
ON-FIELD LOGOS

AS SOON AS a team clinches a spot in the Fall Classic, it's a safe bet that local newspapers will print a photograph of stadium groundskeepers stenciling the World Series logo onto the pennant-winning team's field. Perhaps nothing better signifies that the Fall Classic is on its way.

Although the logo is an intricate design featuring up to six colors, the stenciling process is a simple one. World Class Surfaces of Leland, Miss., has provided teams with stenciling kits for the World Series, Super Bowl and other athletic events for years. Groundskeepers receive one stencil for each color and use water-based paints to fill them in. The process takes about an hour per logo. The paint is durable enough for the logos to withstand any late October precipitation, but has the ability to come off easily when soaked intentionally, allowing for a seamless transition between and after playoff rounds.

Of course, time constraints sometimes cause embarrassing problems. Because teams often want the logos on the field for workout days before the official start of the Series, a seven-game League Championship Series can force teams to act prematurely. Newspapers in New York had a field day running shots of the 2003 World Series logo behind home plate at Fenway Park after the Yankees defeated the Red Sox in Game 7 of that year's ALCS in dramatic fashion.

The grounds crew painted the 2011 World Series logo onto the field during Preview Day at Busch Stadium before St. Louis took on Texas for a shot at the title.

INSIDE THE WORLD SERIES
BATTING PRACTICE

FANS ARRIVING EARLY to a World Series game may be surprised to see a large crowd lingering on the field during batting practice, filling virtually all of the foul territory along the basepaths. Most of the people in the crowd are members of the media or officials from Major League Baseball and its clubs. Unlike the regular season, when there's far less media coverage of any single game and team clubhouses are open for three-hour stretches before contests, access during the postseason is restricted to postgame.

Without permission to enter the clubhouse, the field becomes the only place for the media to congregate and gather information before first pitch. The ability to watch the game's brightest stars take batting practice prior to a game is one of the nicer perks of covering baseball. Because of the sheer number of reporters on the field at this time, though, players and managers rarely stop for interviews, as one question has the potential to turn into a free-for-all.

Although players and managers are mostly unavailable, general managers and front office staff from the participating teams, along with officials from Major League Baseball, its television partners and the MLB Players Association, often take questions during batting practice. It's also the time when any celebrities or dignitaries attending the game might be allowed on the field.

With representatives from so many media outlets on hand, World Series batting practice is a prime networking opportunity. While reporters are there in the hopes that a major interview opportunity arises, a coup like this is rare, and instead media members spend much of their time talking with each other, sharing ideas and anecdotes about the participating clubs.

Media members, along with MLB and team officials, filled AT&T Park's foul territory during BP before the Giants took on the Rangers in the 2010 World Series.

Pregame festivities in Arlington included a flyover before the Rangers took the field against the Giants in Game 5 of the 2010 Fall Classic.

INSIDE THE WORLD SERIES
FLYOVERS

NOTHING ADDS DRAMA and pageantry to a major sporting event quite like a carefully executed military flyover following the singing of the national anthem. To commemorate an event as grand as the World Series, Major League Baseball works with the U.S. military to coordinate flyovers for the Fall Classic, although poor weather conditions and logistical issues, such as close proximity to an airport, can sometimes present a challenge.

Under guidelines established by the Department of Defense, the secretaries of each branch of the armed services determine which events warrant flyovers. MLB, like other professional sports leagues requesting flyovers, must stipulate that the event in question is open to the public, non-political in nature and not a fundraiser for any particular charity.

The military pays for flyovers, which count as training flights for pilots and thus come out of existing budgets. In return, the military receives exposure for recruiting. MLB also provides game tickets to the flight crews, along with World Series souvenirs. Later in the game, the pilots are often shown on in-game video monitors and the TV broadcast.

"We always try to have a flyover for the first home game in each city," said Marla Miller, MLB's senior vice president for special events. "It's just a question of the logistical circumstances we're facing, where the stadium is and weather patterns."

The U.S. Navy's Blue Angels, who have performed aerial demonstrations since 1946, handle many event flyovers, although Miller said MLB also receives requests from the U.S. Army and Air Force. MLB's security department works with the FAA for air clearance in the vicinity of the stadium. Because of the noise generated by the aircraft as they pass over the stadium, clubs make an announcement and show the incoming aircraft on the scoreboard video monitor to prepare fans. The result is breathtaking.

Although post-9/11 security measures prohibit blimps from flying directly over stadiums while shooting footage for TV broadcasts of the World Series, the military faces no such restrictions. In some respects, airspace is less crowded now than it was prior to 9/11, when small planes pulling advertising frequently circled World Series ballparks.

GUEST
Admit to Press Box, Field, Interview Room

Nº 011

NAME HOWARD TALBOT
AFFILIATION HALL OF FAME
GAME 3, 4, 5 DATE 10-20-21-22

NOT TRANSFERABLE
SUBJECT TO CONDITIONS ON REVERSE SIDE
NOT FOR USE BY ANYONE UNDER 18
NO AUTOGRAPHS
ENTER AT PRESS GATE

NAME ED STACK
AFFILIATION HALL OF FAME
This credential must be worn At All Times

WORLD SERIES 1981

ROW SE

1996
World Series
Working Media
Name
Affiliation
Lo

ADMIT
RLD SERIES

STADIUM
ISCONSIN

R. MANN
NEW YORK

N FIELD DURING GAME
OOD FOR ADMISSION

Pass is issued subject to the conditions
set forth on the back hereof

592

7-X

95

1973
WORLD SERIES
SHEA STADIUM
Name
Affiliation
W 598

Name
Affiliation

NOT GOOD
FOR ADMISSION
TO SHEA STADIUM

FIELD
ONLY

WHEN IN USE, THIS BADGE
MUST BE WORN WHERE
IT CAN BE SEEN.

THE FIELD MUST BE VACATED
NUTES PRIOR TO GAME TIME.

1952
WORLD SERIES
Yankee Stadium — New York City
PRESS
Sid Keener
Cooperstown Hall Fame
SEC. 6 AISLE 3
Seat No. 252
Games 1-5
PRESS
(Enter at Press Gate)

1953
WORLD SERIES
Ebbets Field — Brooklyn, N. Y.
WORKING PRESS
Arthur Mann
Dodgers
Section 14 — Row 16 Seat 3
Seat No.
Game 3-4-5-X
(Enter at Press Gate)

INSIDE THE WORLD SERIES
CREDENTIALS

WITH SEVERAL THOUSAND members of the press covering each World Series over the past decade, it's vital that proper credentials are issued. All members of the media, as well as anyone else working the event in an official capacity for Major League Baseball, are issued a credential weeks before the event. This stringent process is for security purposes, but it also facilitates a productive working environment.

Anyone who has received press credentials to cover the World Series has passed muster with John Blundell, MLB's manager of media relations. He oversees credentials for all of baseball's largest events, ranging from the All-Star Game to the World Baseball Classic to MLB's Winter Meetings. But the World Series, typically played in two cities over nearly two weeks, is perhaps the most hectic of all.

About 2,000 press credentials are issued in each city for a typical Fall Classic, more if either New York team or the Boston Red Sox are involved. Many journalists cover games in both cities, although a portion of those based in either of the participating cities attends only home games. Either way, that's a lot of laminated passes, but it represents just a fraction of the applications Blundell receives each year.

MLB prints the credentials at its midtown Manhattan headquarters using protected, watermarked cards. On the front of more recent credentials are the media member's name, affiliation and photo. These passport-sized pictures are printed on the passes to ensure that they are not used by anyone but the intended recipient. The back includes fine-print warnings of the dangers of flying bats and balls, and reminds journalists that autograph seeking is unprofessional and strictly prohibited.

"If you're a legitimate media affiliation, we want you there," Blundell said. "But we have different guidelines for what kind of access you'll receive."

At the press gate, each media member presents identification and receives a credential, a lanyard, tickets to postgame gala receptions and a press pin for each city.

Since space in the clubhouse is limited, even in new ballparks with sprawling facilities, postgame access is capped at about 800 journalists who receive special clubhouse badges. There's a different badge in each city, although some journalists covering the entire postseason receive one for the whole period.

Today, there are fewer newspaper reporters among the ranks, but new media representatives include satellite radio personnel, journalists from the many cable television channels, and those working in the ever-expanding world of online media. With blogs and online baseball websites abounding, Major League Baseball has to draw the line somewhere with credentials. Only those news organizations that have covered MLB through other mainstream media platforms will also receive access for their online reporters.

As professional baseball rosters have become increasingly international, there has also been a boom in interest from media outlets around the world. In 2008, MLB credentialed media members from 23 countries, with Japan representing the largest contingent, as Japanese reporters were on hand to chronicle Akinori Iwamura of the Tampa Bay Rays and So Taguchi of the Philadelphia Phillies. International reporters also recently flocked to the 2013 World Series, in which Japan-born pitcher Koji Uehara helped the Boston Red Sox clinch the title at home with two saves during the Classic.

Mariano Rivera spoke at a press conference after he received the Commissioner's Historic Achievement Award prior to Game 2 of the 2013 Series.

INSIDE THE WORLD SERIES
PRESS CONFERENCES

DURING THE REGULAR season, players and managers generally deal with members of the media in small group sessions in the clubhouse or dugout. But with more than 2,000 press credentials issued for the World Series every year, such access often becomes impossible during the Fall Classic.

Those media members possessing credentials are still granted admittance to the clubhouses after games as they are during the regular season, but no one is allowed in before the contests. To accommodate the heavy media demands before each World Series game, and to lessen the rush afterward, Major League Baseball creates a special interview room in each of the participating ballparks. Here, the managers and select players are brought before reporters for question-and-answer sessions prior to and after games.

The players and managers typically sit on a raised dais in front of a backdrop emblazoned with official World Series and Major League Baseball logos. There's seating for about 200 reporters, and behind them is another raised platform positioned for television cameras.

Katy Feeney and Phyllis Merhige, both senior vice presidents of club relations for Major League Baseball, oversee the interview room and call on reporters for questions. Public relations interns roam the room with microphones so that the questions can be heard by the players and managers, as well as on the live video feeds, which are available to a variety of television networks around the country.

The two executives make it a point to meet every team at the New York ballparks when they come into town during the season, but they also get to know them throughout the postseason by working various press conferences.

"I always joke early on that they have to want to see a lot of me because I'll be there in October," Merhige said.

"If they're lucky, they'll be very sick of us by the end of the month," Feeney added.

The pregame ritual dates back to 1992, when Toronto Blue Jays Manager Cito Gaston asked if he could hold his pregame question-and-answer period in the interview room rather than subject himself to being swarmed on the field during batting practice. Soon, both managers were regularly appearing in the interview room before games, along with the scheduled starting pitchers for the following day's matchup.

The paradox of the interview room is that, in many cases, reporters don't feel inclined to attend since transcripts are provided in the press boxes immediately afterward.

"Sometimes you worry that there won't be enough people there," Feeney said. "And there are times when you have to drag out the first couple of questions."

Tampa Bay Rays Manager Joe Maddon confronted that problem during the 2008 Series by assigning the first question at each of his press conferences to a local radio reporter.

Once each game concludes, public relations officials from both teams escort the managers into the interview room. The losing skipper arrives first to avoid the awkward situation of having to wait in the back of the room while the winning manager speaks. Players from the losing team do not usually come to the interview room to take questions, preferring to speak in the clubhouse.

The winning manager appears next on the dais, and he is generally followed by one or two stars of the game. Those players will likely face another barrage of interrogators once they make their way back to the clubhouse, but at least they've handled the initial onslaught in the interview room.

AT&T PARK

COMMONLY REGARDED AS one of the most picturesque stadiums in all of sports, AT&T Park has quickly become one of many architectural marvels in the Bay Area, and etched itself into baseball lore. In just 15 seasons, the ballpark has already played host to six playoff teams, three World Series championships, the 2007 All-Star Game and a World Baseball Classic final. Among the milestones achieved there are the franchise's first perfect game and MLB's all-time record-breaking home run.

Fans can take the ferry or BART (San Francisco's rail system) to the downtown San Francisco stadium adjacent to the Bay. There, a statue of perhaps the greatest Giant of all time, Willie Mays, greets all those who pass through the main entrance gate. Once inside, fans can take in the brick walls, natural grass playing field and classic, expansive National League dimensions, which give the stadium a nostalgic yet contemporary feel. The ballpark recently added the @Cafe, where fans can enjoy a cup of coffee while engaging in real-time social media conversations about the team.

Although the unmistakable chill of San Francisco still settles in on any given day, the stadium fights the elements much better than its predecessor down at Candlestick Point. At the Giants' old ballpark, the space behind right field was occupied by a bleacher section where kids would gather when Willie McCovey came to the plate. Fans at AT&T Park take to the bay area behind the right-field wall in boats and kayaks in the hopes of catching a home run ball in aptly named McCovey Cove.

BIRTH OF THE GIANTS

ABOUT 3,000 MILES east of San Francisco, and almost 130 years prior to 2014, the Giants entered the baseball world as the New York Gothams of the National League. Founded by tobacco mogul John B. Day and player/manager Jim Mutrie, the Gothams enjoyed great success in the 1880s with two NL pennants and two victories in the pre-modern World Series.

Legend has it that the Gothams became the Giants when Mutrie congratulated his team after a particularly convincing victory by calling his players "my big fellows, my giants." Around the same time, the club moved to upper Manhattan and settled into the Polo Grounds, where it would remain until moving to the West Coast in 1957.

Unlike the 1880s, the following decade was not prosperous for the Giants, who underwent three ownership changes before 1902 and did not finish in first place until 1904. But that year, in his last impactful move before he sold the team, Owner Andrew Freedman hired legendary skipper John McGraw. McGraw managed the Giants for three decades, ushering them to three World Series and two National League pennants.

After memorable moments in the early 1950s, including Bobby Thomson's "Shot Heard 'Round The World" and Willie Mays' "Catch," the Giants relocated to San Francisco in 1957, thus beginning a new era for the franchise and Major League Baseball.

THE 2014
SAN FRANCISCO GIANTS

BRUCE BOCHY
Manager

The winningest active manager in the Majors has led the Giants to three World Series titles in his first eight seasons. The veteran skipper has 20 years of experience, eight of which have been with the San Francisco organization.

COACHING STAFF
Tim Flannery, Third Base Coach
Mark Gardner, Bullpen Coach
Roberto Kelly, First Base Coach
Hensley Meulens, Hitting Coach
Dave Righetti, Pitching Coach
Ron Wotus, Bench Coach

15

EHIRE ADRIANZA
Second Base

This versatile rookie, who hails from Venezuela, played second, third and shortstop for the Giants this season.

6

JEREMY AFFELDT
Pitcher

The 35-year-old reliever did not surrender a run in three separate months during the 2014 campaign. The southpaw was particularly impressive prior to the All-Star break, posting a 1.54 ERA during the first half of the season.

41

JOAQUIN ARIAS
Third Base

Arias, who spent time at all four in-field positions for San Francisco, hit .387 over the regular season's final two months.

13

BRANDON BELT
First Base

Belt's 18th-inning homer lifted the Giants to a Game 2 victory in the NLDS, ending the longest game in postseason history. Despite playing in just 61 games this season due to injury, Belt still managed to launch 12 home runs.

9

GREGOR BLANCO
Outfield

A six-year MLB veteran, Blanco turned up his production in the second half, batting .296 with an .814 OPS. Known for his speed, the outfielder boasted a three-hit game on Sept. 2 and was efficient from the leadoff spot throughout the World Series.

7

GARY BROWN
Outfield

Since his Major League debut on Sept. 3, Brown collected three hits in seven regular-season at-bats. Brown was used primarily as a defensive replacement and a pinch-runner in the Bigs, as he ranked second in the Pacific Coast League with 36 stolen bases for Triple-A Fresno this season.

56

MADISON BUMGARNER
Pitcher

Bumgarner's team-leading 18 wins and 217.1 innings pitched were good enough for fourth among all NL pitchers this season, and he set a career high in innings, wins and strikeouts. He was particularly dominant on the road in 2014, posting a 2.22 ERA with 11 wins and a 0.98 WHIP. Bumgarner carried San Francisco throughout the playoffs, pitching to a 1.42 ERA in the first three series and recording a shutout in the Wild Card Game and the World Series. He was named NLCS MVP for his outstanding efforts.

40

MATT CAIN
Pitcher

Although Matt Cain's season was cut short due to multiple surgeries, he had begun to look like his old All-Star self before hitting the disabled list, amassing 70 K's in 90.1 innings.

18

SANTIAGO CASILLA
Pitcher

The Dominican Republic-born veteran led San Francisco relievers with a 1.70 ERA and 0.86 WHIP, both career bests. After taking over the closer gig mid-season, Casilla tallied 19 saves as the Giants' closer, the second highest total of his 11-year career. He also earned two saves in the NLDS.

46

BRANDON CRAWFORD
Shortstop

Crawford's fourth-inning grand slam in the NL Wild Card Game propelled San Francisco into the NLDS and was the first ever by a shortstop in the postseason. In his fourth year with San Francisco, Crawford set career-high marks in runs, home runs, RBI, slugging and OPS, and tied for the most triples among MLB shortstops (10).

35

MATT DUFFY
Shortstop

The 23-year-old hit .375 in 16 games at AT&T Park after making his Major League debut on May 22. As a rookie, Duffy fared well against southpaws, notching 12 hits in 30 at-bats.

50

JUAN GUTIERREZ
Pitcher

Utilized heavily out of the bullpen, Gutierrez tossed 63.2 innings, good for second most out of all Giants relievers. The Venezuela native recorded his best month in July, pitching to a 1.38 ERA.

57

TIM HUDSON
Pitcher

Hudson, now 39, stormed out of the gate this season, going 4-1 with a 2.17 ERA and 15.5 K/BB ratio in April. The veteran was selected to his fourth career All-Star Game thanks to his torrid start. His 189.1 innings pitched and 3.57 ERA on the season trailed only Madison Bumgarner in San Francisco's rotation.

17

TRAVIS ISHIKAWA
First Base

Ishikawa signed with the Giants in April and filled in at both first base and left field, reaching base at a .333 clip. Ishikawa shined in one of the brightest moments of San Francisco's postseason, as he homered on a 2-0 fastball in the bottom of the ninth inning in Game 5 of the NLCS. His series-clinching shot was just the ninth walk-off home run in history to win a postseason series.

45

TIM LINCECUM
Pitcher

The two-time Cy Young Award winner tossed his second career no-hitter on June 25 against the Padres, proving he still has electric upside. Lincecum, just the second pitcher to throw multiple no-no's against the same team, also pitched in a relief role to end the season and even managed to earn a save in late July.

55

JAVIER LOPEZ
Pitcher

A lefty specialist, Lopez allowed just 18 hits to left-handed batters in the 102 times he faced them this year. He was particularly dominant in July, when he pitched 12 flawless relief appearances.

49

JEAN MACHI
Pitcher

Machi followed up on a stellar rookie season by limiting right-handed opponents to a .186 batting average. The sophomore also tallied seven W's, securing win No. 1 in his first appearance of the season.

63

MICHAEL MORSE
Outfield

The first-year Giant added pop to San Francisco's lineup, leading the club with 14 first-half home runs. But perhaps his most important was an eighth-inning blast in Game 5 of the NLCS, a pinch-hit shot that tied the game and put San Francisco in position to win in the ninth.

38

ANGEL PAGAN
Outfield

Pagan, San Francisco's speedy center fielder, led off for the Giants during much of the season. The table-setter got off to a hot start in 2014, batting .323 with 11 stolen bases through May, before a back injury slowed his pace.

16

JOE PANIK
Second Base

Panik's .305 average was tops among NL rookies. After his late June debut, the youngster had a particularly impressive August, posting a .900 OPS while batting .379 in 25 games. Panik proved to be vital early in the playoffs, as he tallied three hits in the Wild Card Game, and then scored four runs and knocked in five RBI in the subsequent two series.

12

JAKE PEAVY
Pitcher

Peavy took more than 2.50 points off his ERA after joining San Francisco in a midseason trade with Boston. After the All-Star break, the veteran starter posted a 2.17 ERA over 78.2 innings with the Giants, good for a 2.1 WAR.

22

HUNTER PENCE
Outfield

Pence, who played in all 162 games for the second straight season, led the Giants with 180 hits, good for third in the NL. The eight-year veteran, who led all MLB outfielders in at-bats, slugged 20 home runs, stole 13 bases and scored the second-most runs in the National League with 106, a career high. The right fielder also appeared in his third career All-Star Game after scoring 68 runs and batting .296 before the break.

8

JUAN PEREZ
Outfield

After debuting in the summer of 2013, the versatile defender logged time at all three outfield positions this season.

2

YUSMEIRO PETIT
Pitcher

Petit assembled a truly unhittable stretch in July when he retired an MLB-record 46 consecutive batters. He also carried his team to victory in an impressive showing during Game 2 of the NLDS. In the 18-inning affair, Petit tossed six shutout frames in relief, allowing only one hit, and was rewarded for his efforts when San Francisco took the lead in the final frame, securing Petit his first post-season win.

52

BUSTER POSEY
Catcher

The 2012 NL MVP once again impressed, leading all MLB backstops in RBI and average. Posey hit a whopping .354 in the second half, and boosted that to .393 in September, then continued his torrid offense in the NLDS, batting .389. The 27-year-old led by example, placing first or second on his squad in nearly every offensive statistic, including hits, home runs, RBI, runs and OPS.

28

SERGIO ROMO
Pitcher

Romo was dominant after the All-Star break, posting a 0.85 WHIP and a 10.4 K/9 ratio in 24 games. The 2013 team leader in closing out games once again tallied the most saves for the Giants.

54

HECTOR SANCHEZ
Catcher

Sanchez was effective in his fourth season as the backup catcher for the Giants. The backstop also logged his first and only career start at first base on May 13. Sanchez added 32 hits with 28 RBI before going on the DL.

29

PABLO SANDOVAL
Third Base

In his sixth full season, Sandoval ranked among the top five NL third basemen in hits, average, slugging, homers, RBI and runs. Panda slugged career homer No. 100 in July in front of his home crowd. Sandoval was electric throughout October, posting a .326 average and .396 OBP in the first three series, adding to his already impressive career postseason resume.

48

HUNTER STRICKLAND
Pitcher

The hard-throwing rookie struck out more than a batter per inning and registered a 0.71 WHIP in nine regular-season games. In Game 2 of the NLDS, Strickland recorded the save in the 18th inning of the longest game in postseason history.

60

ANDREW SUSAC
Catcher

A 24-year-old freshman, Susac hit .333 with a .444 OBP in 36 plate appearances against left-handers this season. He's a steady defender that has shown raw power during the early stages of his Big League career.

34

RYAN VOGELSONG
Pitcher

Vogelsong pitched 5.2 innings of two-hit ball in Game 4 of the Division Series to help the Giants clinch an NLCS berth. In his sixth season with the Giants, the veteran was top-notch at AT&T Park, where he held batters to a .228 average.

32

2014
THE SEASON IN REVIEW

"GOOD PITCHING beats good hitting." It's a phrase that baseball fans have heard and pondered for decades. In 2014, this theory was once again put to the test in a year when pitching was remarkable and hitting became all the more sought after.

The 2014 season brought with it the most shutouts since 1972. It saw a spike in strikeouts and a drop in ERA. It featured five no-hitters, spun by both veterans and young guns, as well as MLB's 2 millionth strikeout and the fastest pitch ever recorded by a starting pitcher. Yet fans also got to witness game-winning grand slams, milestone home runs and the final at-bats of baseball's Mr. November.

As it stands, the question of whether a knee-buckling curveball from Clayton Kershaw can consistently overcome the bat speed and instincts of Mike Trout is still up for debate. What isn't, though, is that in 2014, both stellar pitching and superb hitting thrilled fans from coast to coast.

Cruz (above left) and Wainwright (above right) were two of the stars of the MLB season. In Kansas City, Ventura emerged as a stud hurler himself, tying for the club lead in wins while delivering 100-mph fastballs.

THE SEASON IN REVIEW
BEST OF 2014

EN ROUTE TO their second franchise Wild Card berth, the Giants sported a combination of fresh talent and successful mainstays. Ace **Madison Bumgarner** led the pitching staff alongside free agent signee Tim Hudson in a rotation that, with St. Louis, boasted the most complete games in MLB. San Francisco staples like **Buster Posey** and Pablo "Kung Fu Panda" Sandoval continued to excite, supported by effective newcomers like power bat Michael Morse, journeyman Travis Ishikawa and rookie Joe Panik.

Together, this mix of old and new formed a Giants team that surprised and impressed. Fans witnessed a range of spectacles, from Tim Lincecum hurling his second career no-hitter to rookie Hunter Strickland picking up his first save. San Francisco's season featured the perfect blend.

FINAL STANDINGS

AMERICAN LEAGUE

EAST	W	L	GB
xBaltimore	96	66	-
New York	84	78	12
Toronto	83	79	13
Tampa Bay	77	85	19
Boston	71	91	25

CENTRAL	W	L	GB
xDetroit	90	72	-
yKansas City	89	73	1
Cleveland	85	77	5
Chicago	73	89	17
Minnesota	70	92	20

WEST	W	L	GB
xLos Angeles	98	64	-
yOakland	88	74	10
Seattle	87	75	11
Houston	70	92	28
Texas	67	95	31

NATIONAL LEAGUE

EAST	W	L	GB
xWashington	96	66	-
Atlanta	79	83	17
New York	79	83	17
Miami	77	85	19
Philadelphia	73	89	23

CENTRAL	W	L	GB
xSt. Louis	90	72	-
yPittsburgh	88	74	2
Milwaukee	82	80	8
Cincinnati	76	86	14
Chicago	73	89	17

WEST	W	L	GB
xLos Angeles	94	68	-
ySan Francisco	88	74	6
San Diego	77	85	17
Colorado	66	96	28
Arizona	64	98	30

x Division winner; y Wild Card

CATEGORY LEADERS

AMERICAN LEAGUE

Batting Average	Jose Altuve, Houston	.341
Hits	Jose Altuve, Houston	225
Home Runs	Nelson Cruz, Baltimore	40
RBI	Mike Trout, Los Angeles	111
Stolen Bases	Jose Altuve, Houston	56
Wins	Corey Kluber, Cleveland Max Scherzer, Detroit Jered Weaver, Los Angeles	18
ERA	Felix Hernandez, Seattle	2.14
Strikeouts	David Price, Detroit	271
Saves	Fernando Rodney, Seattle	48

NATIONAL LEAGUE

Batting Average	Justin Morneau, Colorado	.319
Hits	Ben Revere, Philadelphia Denard Span, Washington	184
Home Runs	Giancarlo Stanton, Miami	37
RBI	Adrian Gonzalez, Los Angeles	116
Stolen Bases	Dee Gordon, Los Angeles	64
Wins	Clayton Kershaw, Los Angeles	21
ERA	Clayton Kershaw, Los Angeles	1.77
Strikeouts	Johnny Cueto, Cincinnati Stephen Strasburg, Wash.	242
Saves	Craig Kimbrel, Atlanta	47

CHECK THE TAPE

THE FIRST USE of instant replay took place on March 31 in a matchup between the Cubs and Pirates. Chicago Manager Rick Renteria, who led MLB skippers in 2014 challenges, contested a double play call, but after review, the call on the field stood, and Jeff Samardzija remained out at first.

YU DID IT

RANGERS ACE Yu Darvish became the fastest pitcher ever to reach 500 career K's on April 6. Darvish has dominated hitters since his rookie season, striking out more than 11 opponents per nine innings.

NEED FOR SPEED

ON APRIL 9, 23-year-old Kansas City rookie Yordano Ventura threw the fastest pitch ever recorded by a starter during the regular season. The hurler's 102.9-mph fastball actually broke his own record from last year. Ventura is a key cog in a young rotation that was largely responsible for the Royals' resurgence in 2014.

WHEN THE San Francisco Giants signed longtime Braves pitcher **Tim Hudson** this offseason, they were looking for a reliable competitor who could stabilize the rotation. Hudson proved to be all that and more, putting together possibly his best season in three years and slotting behind Madison Bumgarner in the rotation after Matt Cain's season was cut short due to multiple surgeries. On April 2, the 38-year-old threw seven innings of shutout ball in his Giants debut, securing his first win.

Hudson got even better as the first half progressed. In April, he earned four wins and posted a 2.17 ERA, and the latter mark dropped even further after he put up a 1.46 ERA in May. The veteran earned a trip to the All-Star Game at Target Field in July, and proved to be a formidable force atop the Giants' staff.

THE SEASON IN REVIEW
MAY

A STATELY VISIT

ON MAY 22, President **Barack Obama** became the first sitting president to visit the Baseball Hall of Fame. The commander in chief, a White Sox devotee, told fans in Cooperstown, N.Y., "I love baseball. America loves baseball."

REDBIRD ON A ROLL

ADAM WAINWRIGHT won his first career Player of the Week Award on May 27 thanks to a stretch in which he threw his first-ever one-hit shutout and combined for 17 scoreless innings with 21 K's. Wainwright's early-season performance earned him a second-straight All-Star nod, and he started the game for the NL.

ZACK ATTACK

ON MAY 16, Zack Greinke gave up two runs or fewer in his 21st straight start, the longest streak of its kind since 1914. The hurler's incredible run dated back to July 2013 and cemented Greinke's status as a force atop a potent Dodgers rotation.

PABLO SANDOVAL has provided muscle and an impressive batting average out of the Giants' hot corner for six years, and "Kung Fu Panda" flipped on the power switch again early this season. On May 29, Sandoval hit his sixth home run of the month, the most that he would tally for any 30-game stretch during the season. He crushed right-handed pitching all year to the tune of 11 home runs, 54 RBI, a .317 average and a .461 slugging percentage. That night was no different, as he launched a third-pitch change-up from southpaw Jaime Garcia over the center-field wall.

Sandoval enjoyed his best month of the season in May, when he put up a .312/.333/.532 slash line. Hunter Pence benefited from hitting in front of Sandoval in 2014, as many of his 106 runs scored were a result of Panda's proficiency at the plate.

CLUTCH CUTCH

ON JUNE 13 at Citi Field, **Andrew McCutchen** made an outstanding catch, running 83 feet and topping out at 19.4 mph to take away a surefire double. According to MLB Advanced Media's player tracking system, the reigning National League MVP's route efficiency was 99.7 percent.

BYE BYE BIRDIE

ON JUNE 25, Nelson Cruz delivered a game-tying grand slam with two outs in the eighth inning to propel the Orioles to victory. Cruz's shot may have been just the spark that Baltimore needed, as the Orioles surpassed the Blue Jays for sole possession of the AL East one week later, a spot they would keep until they clinched the division title in September.

MR. PADRE

TONY GWYNN, the legendary Mr. Padre, passed away on June 16 at age 54. The Hall of Famer was one of MLB's all-time greats, collecting eight batting titles and appearing in 15 All-Star Games during his 20 Big League seasons. Gwynn finished with 3,141 career hits, good for 19th all time.

EVEN DURING A bumpy season, **Tim Lincecum** showed Giants fans that he still has true lights-out stuff. In a June 25 contest against the San Diego Padres, Lincecum tossed his second career no-hitter, striking out six and giving up only one free pass. After walking Chase Headley in the second inning, he retired the next 23 batters to become just the second pitcher in Major League history to no-hit the same team twice, joining Hall of Famer Addie Joss.

Throughout the season, Lincecum proved willing to help San Francisco make the playoffs by any means necessary, even if that meant taking on a less familiar role. Lincecum was asked to pitch out of the bullpen in late August, swapping duties with right-hander Yusmeiro Petit. He managed to earn a save while Petit threw a complete game during the regular season's final month.

JULY

PUT IT IN THE BOOKS

CLEVELAND'S **Danny Salazar** struck out Kansas City's Nori Aoki on July 27 at Kauffman Stadium to record the 2 millionth strikeout in Major League Baseball history. Strikeout totals have increased every year since 2005.

FLAME THROWER

IN A JULY 28 contest against the Diamondbacks, Cincinnati's **Aroldis Chapman** threw 15 pitches that clocked in at 101 mph or higher. The flame-throwing reliever, who battled back from a preseason injury, also extended his Major League record for most consecutive relief appearances with a strikeout to 44.

TARGET PRACTICE

THE 2014 HOME RUN DERBY was held at Target Field, and **Yoenis Cespedes** won the crown for the second straight year, with his longest home run flying 452 feet. He out-hit Todd Frazier in the finals, mashing nine long-balls to Frazier's lone blast to defend his title. All in all, 79 homers left the ballpark that night.

THE NAME Buster Posey is synonymous with San Francisco success — he was on both the 2010 and 2012 World Series rosters — and the catcher continued to lead the Giants to victory in 2014. In a July 13 game, he again proved why he is one of MLB's best behind the plate. While Madison Bumgarner and Posey had definite chemistry on the mound and at home plate, they were determined to match each other offensively, as well. In an unusual twist, the pair became the first batterymates to hit grand slams in the same game.

After the All-Star break, Posey thrust himself into the MVP conversation by batting .354 with 12 homers down the stretch. Not only did he end up leading all catchers in average, slugging percentage, RBI and OPS, but he also posted the second highest WAR of any catcher, behind only Milwaukee's Jonathan Lucroy.

WALK THAT WAY

ON AUG. 21, the Nationals won their second consecutive game in walk-off fashion, capping an impressive string of 10 straight wins. This run, sparked by an offense that boasted the likes of Adam LaRoche, Bryce Harper and Denard Span, included five walk-off wins in total, and catapulted Washington to its second National League East title in three years.

THE KING'S REIGN

ON AUG. 11, **Felix Hernandez** completed his 16th consecutive start in which he pitched seven or more innings and allowed two or fewer runs. During that record-setting stretch, which bested Tom Seaver's previous mark, King Felix led the Mariners to a minuscule 2.50 team ERA.

NO SMALL FEAT

ON AUG. 28, San Francisco's **Yusmeiro Petit** retired his 46th straight batter, securing the longest streak in history for any pitcher.

WHEN Madison Bumgarner is on the mound, the Giants have complete confidence that their ace will lead them to victory. On Aug. 26, the fans at AT&T Park were treated to a spectacle, as Bumgarner pitched the best game of his career. The only blemish preventing perfection? A single hit, off the bat of Justin Morneau in the eighth inning. Bumgarner tried to throw a low curveball, but veter-an Morneau just managed to get a piece of it and lofted the pitch into right field for a double.

Before that hit, Bumgarner retired 21 straight batters and struck out 13 without allowing a walk. It was another stellar moment during a fantastic season for the young Giants ace, a campaign that saw him total 18 wins, four complete games, a 2.98 ERA and 219 strikeouts.

A TRIPLE DOUBLE

ON SEPT. 13, Ian Desmond became the third shortstop in MLB history to have three 20-homer, 20-steal seasons in a row. Desmond has flashed exceptional speed and power for a shortstop, acting as a catalyst in the middle of a dominant Nationals lineup.

BELTWAY PRIDE

THE BALTIMORE ORIOLES clinched their first division title in 17 years on Sept. 16, ending one of MLB's longest droughts. With the Washington Nationals winning that evening, as well, the date also marked the third time since 1969 that two MLB teams from the same metro area have clinched on the same night.

ALL IN THE FAMILY

ALSO ON SEPT. 13, Brett Bochy made history in his Major League debut as the first pitcher ever to take the ball from his own father on a Big League mound. Bruce Bochy, the San Francisco Giants' manager, called upon his son to help the team out of a bases-loaded jam.

FOR Hunter Pence, days off are hard to come by — and he likes it that way. Through late September, Pence had played in 331 consecutive games, yet he wasn't in the outfield on Sept. 27 to start game No. 332. The Giants had just clinched a spot in the playoffs, and management wanted to give Pence a day to rest before the long playoff journey ahead. Not wanting to remain dormant, however, he managed to make his way into the game as a pinch-hitter in the seventh inning.

A versatile asset in the San Francisco lineup, Pence led all MLB outfielders in at-bats this season, slugged 20 home runs, stole 13 bases and scored 106 runs. After setting a career high in home runs and steals last year, he recorded a new personal best in runs scored while pacing the Giants in hits in 2014.

ZEROED IN

DESPITE THE SKILL that pitchers displayed in 2014, the no-hitter remained as elusive and exciting as ever. But fans at five games were lucky enough to witness one. The first was thrown by veteran Josh Beckett, who weaved his gem for L.A. in May before retiring after the season. Then Clayton Kershaw twirled his first career no-hitter in mid-June, striking out 15 batters in the process. Next, San Francisco's Tim Lincecum dazzled against the Padres, throwing the second no-hitter of his career. The fourth was a group effort begun by the Phillies' Cole Hamels and finished by Ken Giles, Jake Diekman and Jonathan Papelbon. The last gem was spun by Washington's **Jordan Zimmermann**, who tossed the first no-no in Nationals history on the final day of the season.

BENCHMARKS OF SUCCESS

SOME OF BASEBALL'S most talented veterans reached new career thresholds in 2014. In April, Detroit's Miguel Cabrera homered for his 2,000th hit. Also that month, the Angels' **Albert Pujols** joined the 500–home run club, launching bombs Nos. 499 and 500 on the same night. And Adrian Beltre proved yet again that talent trumps age, tallying career hit No. 2,500 at 35.

FITTING FINALE

THE SCRIPT COULD not have been written any better. In the bottom of the ninth of his final game at Yankee Stadium, **Derek Jeter** came to the plate with a man on second and pride on the line. In thrilling fashion, he slapped the first pitch he saw into right field, delivering an appropriately dramatic walk-off win.

MOST DOMINANT PLAYERS

THE 2014 CAMPAIGN was ripe with Major Leaguers who proved themselves as the world's greatest ballplayers at the plate, in the field or on the mound over the course of 162 ballgames. Each player on this list stands out for an extraordinary accomplishment (or many). Clayton Kershaw tops our countdown, rounded out by some of the greatest pitchers, hardest hitters and strongest fielders of 2014.

1. CLAYTON KERSHAW
PITCHER, LOS ANGELES DODGERS

The highlight of Kershaw's season came on June 18, when he threw his first career no-hitter, striking out 15 Rockies. The outing was part of the ace's stunning streak of 41 scoreless innings that continued through July 10, MLB's 15th-longest scoreless innings streak at the time.

The left-hander racked up his fifth-straight season with 200-plus K's, and on Sept. 19, Kershaw became the first hurler with 20 wins this season, and just the second player to reach the mark in fewer than 30 starts since World War II.

2. MIKE TROUT
OUTFIELD, LOS ANGELES ANGELS

By WAR, Trout was the best position player ever through his age-22 season. "He hits for power, average and gets those bases," says Astros DH Chris Carter. "He does it all."

The slugger's work at the All-Star Game earned him the game's MVP Award for a performance the likes of which have not been seen since 1934. Trout became the first player with at least a double, triple and two RBI in the Midsummer Classic since Earl Averill did so 80 years ago.

Kershaw, just the fifth Dodgers pitcher to make four consecutive Opening Day starts, put up an MVP–worthy display on the mound in 2014.

Trout led the AL in RBI while vying for the MVP Award for the third consecutive season.

3. MIGUEL CABRERA
FIRST BASE, DETROIT TIGERS

Miggy started off the season by signing an eight-year contract extension with the Tigers and launching a home run for his 2,000th career hit. In May, the two-time AL MVP tallied his 1,300th RBI, becoming just the seventh Big Leaguer to reach the mark in his first 12 seasons.

Cabrera homered in the All-Star Game this summer, making him the first Tiger to do so since Lou Whitaker in 1986. "I'm honored to play on the same team as him," says Tigers infielder Nick Castellanos. "He makes me want to get better and shows me what I can be like."

4. FELIX HERNANDEZ
PITCHER, SEATTLE MARINERS

From May to August, Seattle's ace posted 16 consecutive starts in which he allowed no more than two runs over at least seven innings, setting a new MLB record. On Aug. 11, the AL Cy Young Award contender became the youngest pitcher to reach the 2,000-inning mark since Dwight Gooden did so in '93.

5. GIANCARLO STANTON
OUTFIELD, MIAMI MARLINS

Stanton began April with a 484-foot homer, but his most impressive blast came in the Home Run Derby, when he launched a 510-foot moonshot into Target Field's upper deck. When the 24-year-old hit his 150th career longball this summer, he became the 10th-youngest Major Leaguer to accomplish the feat. Despite suffering a brutal injury after taking a pitch to the face on Sept. 11, Stanton still stood out as one of the NL's top MVP candidates.

6. CRAIG KIMBREL
PITCHER, ATLANTA BRAVES

In June, Kimbrel notched his 155th career save to become the Braves' all-time leader. In August, he was the first pitcher in his league to reach 40 saves. The closer also was the second-fastest reliever ever to arrive at 180 career saves. Kimbrel represents the only player in MLB history to garner 40-plus saves in each of his first four full seasons.

Sandoval joined Albert Pujols, Reggie Jackson and Babe Ruth when he hit an MLB record three homers in one game during the 2012 Fall Classic.

run off Brad Lidge in the bottom of the frame. The left fielder propelled the White Sox to a walk-off victory, and Chicago would go on to sweep the Fall Classic.

2009 New York Yankees

After falling to the Phillies in Game 1 behind Cliff Lee's masterful pitching, New York needed a win before the Series left Yankee Stadium. A.J. Burnett delivered, allowing just one run over seven frames in a 3-1 Yankees win to even the Fall Classic at one game apiece.

New York took two of three in Philadelphia to send Game 6 back to the Bronx. There, World Series MVP Hideki Matsui drilled a two-run homer in the second inning before adding a two-run single in the third and a two-run double in the fifth to tie the single-game Fall Classic record for RBI with six. In the end, it was the incomparable Mariano Rivera who pitched the final 1.2 innings in front of the raucous home crowd to seal the Yankees' 27th world title.

2010 San Francisco Giants

In Game 1 of the 2010 World Series, the Giants found themselves up against an early 2-0 deficit at home while facing the Rangers. But San Francisco battled back and took the lead during a six-run fifth inning, highlighted by a three-run Juan Uribe longball. The Giants went on to win, 11-7.

San Francisco's bats stayed hot in Game 2, and Matt Cain pitched 7.2 scoreless innings for a 9-0 victory and a 2-0 Series lead. The Giants would fall in Game 3 before beating the Rangers the next two times out to earn the franchise's sixth title.

2011 St. Louis Cardinals

The 2011 Fall Classic began as a back-and-forth affair, and Game 5 opened in Arlington with the Series knotted, 2 games to 2. When the Cardinals dropped that contest, they found themselves facing a must-win Game 6. But, the Series then shifted back to St. Louis, where magic ensued.

Down two runs with two outs in the bottom of the ninth, Series MVP David Freese hit a game-tying triple. After Texas regained the lead in the 10th, St. Louis tied it again in the bottom of the frame, before Freese hit a walk-off home run in the 11th to keep his club alive.

In the deciding Game 7, Allen Craig's third-inning longball gave the Cardinals a lead they would never relinquish. Jason Motte pitched a perfect ninth, and St. Louis celebrated on its home field at Busch Stadium.

2012 San Francisco Giants

As with previous teams owning home-field advantage, the Giants used big and early home runs to pace a Game 1 victory. But this time, all of the roundtrippers came from one man: Pablo Sandoval. The third baseman went deep three times, in the first, third and fifth innings, to tie a World Series record as San Francisco topped Detroit, 8-3, at AT&T Park.

The home crowd didn't witness quite the same fireworks in Game 2, but ultimately got the result it was looking for. This time, the Giants used pitching to stymie the Tigers in a 2-0 victory, as Madison Bumgarner and two relievers combined to toss a two-hit shutout, allowing the club to leave the Bay Area with a two-game Series lead.

San Francisco took the next two contests in Detroit en route to a Fall Classic sweep and its second World Series title in just three seasons.

2007 and 2013 Boston Red Sox

After capturing their first title in 86 years in 2004, the Red Sox were hungry for more in '07. In a deja vu moment that evoked memories of their World Series run three years earlier, a Sox batter belted a first-inning homer in Game 1. On this occasion, it came off the bat of leadoff hitter Dustin Pedroia in a 13-1 romp over the Colorado Rockies. Boston would sweep the Series to earn its second title of the decade.

The Red Sox got off to a quick start again in 2013, scoring three runs in the first inning of a Game 1 victory over the Cardinals. After falling in Game 2, Boston took two of the three contests in St. Louis before heading back to New England for a deciding Game 6.

There, John Lackey hurled 6.2 innings of one-run ball as the Red Sox clinched their first World Series title at Fenway Park since 1918.

Ortiz (top) came up big in the Red Sox's 2004 Fall Classic sweep, launching a three-run, Game 1 longball. Konerko's Game 2 grand slam made the difference for the White Sox a year later.

SAN FRANCISCO GIANTS
2014 MINOR LEAGUE RESULTS

AAA FRESNO GRIZZLIES (68-76)

4th in Pacific Coast League Pacific Northern Division

AA RICHMOND FLYING SQUIRRELS (79-63)

1st in Eastern League Western Division

HIGH-A SAN JOSE GIANTS (73-67)

4th in California League North Division

CLASS-A AUGUSTA GREENJACKETS (62-76)

4th in South Atlantic League Southern Division

CLASS-A SHORT SEASON SALEM-KEIZER VOLCANOES (38-38)

3rd in Northwest League South Division

ROOKIE AZL GIANTS (34-22)

1st in Arizona League East Division

ROOKIE DSL GIANTS (46-23)

2nd in Dominican Summer League Boca Chica South Division

MAJOR LEAGUE BASEBALL PROPERTIES

Senior Vice President, Consumer Products	HOWARD SMITH
Vice President, Publishing	DONALD S. HINTZE
Editorial Director	MIKE McCORMICK
Publications Art Director	FAITH M. RITTENBERG
Senior Production Manager	CLAIRE WALSH
Senior Account Executive, Publishing	CHRIS RODDAY
Senior Publishing Coordinator	JAKE SCHWARTZSTEIN
Associate Art Director	MARK CALIMBAS
Associate Editor	ALLISON DUFFY
Project Assistant Editors	DANA ROSE FALCONE
	ANDREW SHELDON
Project Designer	JENIFER COZZOLINO
Editorial Intern	JOE SPARACIO

MAJOR LEAGUE BASEBALL PHOTOS

Manager	JESSICA FOSTER
Photo Editor	JIM McKENNA
Project Photo Editor	TAYLOR BAUCOM

WORLD SERIES
CONTRIBUTING PHOTOGRAPHERS
Brad Mangin
Rob Tringali
Ron Vesely

THE FENN / McCLELLAND & STEWART TEAM

Publisher, FENN	C. JORDAN FENN
President & CEO	BRAD MARTIN
President & Publisher, RHC	KRISTIN COCHRANE
Executive Managing Editor	ELIZABETH KRIBS
EVP, Director of Production	JANINE LAPORTE
Senior Production Coordinator	CHRISTIE HANSON
EVP, Director of Sales	DUNCAN SHIELDS
Director of Sales	JAMES YOUNG
Publicity Manager	RUTA LIORMONAS
Manager, Online Marketing	JESSICA SCOTT
Director, Special Promotions and Marketing	RANDY CHAN

Ron Vesely/MLB Photos: Front Cover; Back Cover (Posey & Bumgarner); 8 (Bumgarner); 12-13; 32; 53; 56 (Blanco); 58 (Sluggerrr); 66 (Posey & Strickland); 67; 72 (Sandoval); 76 (Crawford); 77; 79; 154

Brad Mangin/MLB Photos: Back Cover (Sandoval); 4 (Sandoval); 9 (jersey); 9 (crowd); 11 (Blanco); 14 (baseballs); 15 (Posey, celebration); 52; 54 (3); 55; 56 (Blanco); 59; 62 (Crawford); 65; 70; 71; 75; 76 (Sandoval); 78; 80; 86; 90-91; 99; 103; 108-109; 110; 122-123; 126-127; 128 (Sanchez); 137; 156; 158

Rob Tringali/MLB Photos: Back Cover (Pence); 6-7; 9 (fans); 10 (warm-ups); 11 (boats); 14 (fountain, dog); 15 (helmets); 22; 23 (2); 58 (Infante); 60; 61; 62 (fan); 63; 64; 66 (Morse); 96; 98 (McCovey Cove) 118; 134 (Darvish); 138 (McCutchen); 141; 147; 150-151; 152

Joe Sargent/MLB Photos: 4 (Bumgarner); 20; 21; 133

Christian Peterson/Getty Images: 5; 48 (Sandoval); 51 (Bumgarner, Group); 103 (Adrianza)

Jamie Squire/Getty Images: 8 (fans); 34; 36; 37; 102

Michael Zagaris/MLB Photos: 69

Patrick Smith/Getty Images: 24 (Sandoval); 25

Rob Carr/Getty Images: 24 (Petit); 68 (Confetti)

Thearon W. Henderson/Getty Images: 26; 40; 45; 49; 104; 107; 113 (Duffy); 114; 117 (2); 121; 124; 128 (Romo); 131; 142 (Petit); 143; 144 (Bochy)

Jed Jacobsohn/MLB Photos: 27; 28; 30; 31; 119; 125; 129; 130 (Strickland); 148-149

Ezra Shaw/Getty Images: 29 (2); 41 (Jay); 42; 103 (Affeldt); 106

Dilip Vishwanat/Getty Images: 33; 35; 57; 134 (Ventura)

John Todd/MLB Photos: 38; 39; 41 (celebration)

Harry How/Getty Images: 43; 44; 105; 136 (Greinke)

Jason O. Watson/Getty Images: 46; 116; 120; 139

John Storey/MLB Photos: 47; 48 (Morse); 50; 51 (clubhouse)

Elsa/Getty Images: 58 (Sandoval); 68 (Williams)

Doug Pensinger/Getty Images: 72 (Vogelsong)

Library of Congress: 82

NBLA/MLB Photos: 83; 84; 94 (1952, 1953, 1958, 1973, 1981, 1987)

New York Daily News Archive/Getty Images: 85

Rich Pilling/MLB Photos: 88-89; 92-93; 158

MLB Photos: 94 (1996)

Ralph Freso/MLB Photos: 111; 135; 145

Paul Spinelli/MLB Photos: 112; 113 (Gutierrez)

Norm Hall/Getty Images: 115

Brian Bahr/Getty Images: 130 (Susac)

Mitchell Layton/Getty Images: 132 (Cruz); 138 (Cruz); 144 (Orioles); 146 (Zimmermann)

Andy Lyons/Getty Images: 132 (Wainwright)

Ed Zurga/Getty Images: 132 (Ventura); 140 (Salazar)

Gene Puskar/AP Photo: 134 (review)

John Grieshop/MLB Photos: 136 (Wainwright)

Milo Stewart Jr./NBLA/MLB Photos: 136 (Obama)

Denis Poroy/Getty Images: 138 (Gwynn)

Jamie Sabau/Getty Images: 140 (Chapman)

Sara Rubinstein/MLB Photos: 140 (Cespedes)

Rey Del Rio/MLB Photos: 142 (Hernandez)

Win McNamee/Getty Images: 142 (Nationals)

Andy Marlin/Getty Images: 144 (Desmond)

Mitchell Layton/MLB Photos: 146 (Pujols)

Joe Robbins/Getty Images: 153 (Stanton)

Otto Greule Jr./Getty Images: 153 (Hernandez)